THINGS VISIBLE AND INVISIBLE

THINGS VISIBLE AND INVISIBLE

*Images in the Spirituality of
St. Catherine of Siena*

GIULIANA CAVALLINI

Translated by
SISTER MARY JEREMIAH, OP
Monastery of the Infant Jesus

ALBA·HOUSE   NEW·YORK

SOCIETY OF ST. PAUL, 2187 VICTORY BLVD., STATEN ISLAND, NEW YORK 10314

Originally published in Italian by the Centro Nazionale di Studi
Cateriniani, Rome, under the title *Le cose visibili e invisibili.*

Library of Congress Cataloging-in-Publication Data

Cavallini, Giuliana.
   Things visible and invisible: images in the spirituality of St.
Catherine of Siena / Giuliana Cavallini: translated by Sister Mary
Jeremiah.
     p.   cm.
   Includes bibliographical references.
   ISBN 0-8189-0733-9
   1. Catherine of Siena, Saint, 1347-1380.   2. Spirituality —
History — Middle Ages, 600-1500.   I. Title.
BX4700.C4C35   1996
282'.092 — dc20   95-51322
                                      CIP

Produced and designed in the United States of America by the
Fathers and Brothers of the Society of St. Paul,
2187 Victory Boulevard, Staten Island, New York 10314,
as part of their communications apostolate.

ISBN: 0-8189-0733-9

Printing Information:

Current Printing - first digit 1 2 3 4 5 6 7 8 9 10

Year of Current Printing - first year shown

| 1996 | 1997 | 1998 | 1999 | 2000 | 2001 |

*This is the great dignity
to see in God,
that whoever would have light
and knowledge of his greatness,
finds it in
things visible and invisible.
(Letter 39)*

TABLE OF CONTENTS

FOREWORD

One could say all the evil that one wishes about this book, if it would be helpful. One could say that there is no critical sense; that the chronology has not been considered and, therefore, neither has it been respected; that comparisons have frequently and freely been made between the pertinent texts taken from very different moments in Catherine's life when she wrote them.

It is all true! It is so obvious that it is useless to discuss it. Some enjoy criticizing a serious, critical and erudite work, but here there is no pretense of this type.

What is this then? Nothing but a fantasy. It is a fantasy freely recreating the circumstances that could have given rise to some of the images in Catherine's mind which made her words live. Some images, not all, so as not to fall into the heavy pedantry of a list.

It is a free fantasy, but not unbridled. Granted it is arbitrary in relating thoughts and historical circumstances of the life of the saint from Siena, but without ever trespassing into the field of probable logic. Just to give an example: it has in no way been proved that one of the Benincasa household was ill that Holy Thursday on which she wrote the letter "To the Prisoners," but it is very certain that Catherine did not learn the technique of administering medicine through a mother's milk from a treatise on pediatrics.

We leave those who have good and strong teeth to taste St. Catherine's words in the original writing — the letters and *The Dialogue*. This little book is offered to all those, and there are many, who are aware of possessing "baby teeth."

The passages presented are, at least in quantity and scope, limited by discretion. But the references are always indicated so that those who wish to know more will be able easily to find the place from which the citations are taken.

Persons of the most diverse conditions approached Catherine of Siena during her lifetime. Often they were animated not by admiration but by hostile sentiments: old men hardened in hatred, sworn enemies of peace and concord; young people who came to her in order to please a friend, but decided not to let her take them from a life of pleasure and sin; professors of theology, jealous of the doctrine of that illiterate woman; spiritually mediocre people unnerved by her flights of the eagle. No one ever succeeded in resisting her. No one approached her without becoming better for it.

Foreword

Today, in the absence of Catherine's living voice, her written words remain for us. They too can make us better for penetrating them. And so, this book. Catherine, who is too great to scorn humble things, can use it to attract the timid to herself. It will be, to employ one of her images, as a hook thrown out to anyone who passes by. If someone will bite it, she will be led — it is hoped — by the clear water of catherinian doctrine to that "Fountain of First Truth" where the soul, gazing upon the Love that created and redeemed her, knows her own beauty and dignity, and falls in love.

Giuliana Cavallini
Rome, Italy

A BRIEF LIFE OF
ST. CATHERINE OF SIENA

Catherine of Siena was born in 1347, the 24th of the 25 children of Jacopo and Lapa Benincasa. In 1354, at the age of 7, Catherine made a private vow of virginity. When she was 15, in 1362, she rejected a marriage arranged by her family. The resulting period of tension and estrangement lasted about a year, until Jacopo relented and let his daughter follow her own path.

In 1364 or 1365, Catherine joined the Sisters of Penance of Saint Dominic, a Dominican third order of laywomen also called the Mantellate. In the following years, Catherine grew spiritually, attracted followers, and met with opposition from some Dominicans and Mantellates.

In 1374, Catherine attended the Dominican General Chapter in Florence, where Raymond of Capua, her future biographer, was assigned as her confessor.

Catherine gained fame as a mystic and as a spiritual teacher. Her followers included men and women, priests, religious and laity. She began to exercise considerable influence on public affairs.

In 1376, Catherine went to Avignon in southern France, where the popes had lived for nearly 70 years. She urged Pope Gregory XI to return to Rome, which he did in 1377, dying the following year. What followed, however, was the Great Schism, a period of some 40 years during which there was a pope in Avignon as well as in Rome. During this time, even saints and theologians were divided as to which person was the legitimate pope.

Although Catherine was not completely illiterate, as has sometimes been claimed, she dictated her works. Besides her many letters, her major work was the *Dialogue*, which she worked on from 1377 to 1378.

Catherine died in 1380. Raymond of Capua began writing his biography of her 5 years later, drawing on his conversations with and recollections of her, on her writings, and on the recollections of her family, friends, and co-workers. She was canonized in 1461, and was declared a Doctor of the Church by Pope Paul VI in 1970.

These are a few of the exterior facts of the life of Catherine of Siena. They may help the reader to better understand the context of Catherine's interior life, which is treated in the following pages. Readers wishing to learn more about Catherine's life and teachings can find a reliable guide in *My Nature is Fire: Saint Catherine of Siena*, by Catherine M. Meade, CSJ (Alba House, 1991).

Bro. Frank Sadowski, SSP
Staten Island, NY

THINGS VISIBLE AND INVISIBLE

CHAPTER ONE

THE FOUNTAIN AND THE VESSEL

Whoever goes from St. Catherine's house down towards the Piatta Valley, finds a low battlement construction on the right: Fontebranda. If you want to draw water you have to descend from the street level to the lower part and look through the large pointed arches over the spring. And if, before entering, you pause and look up the hill, you can see standing out against the sky the massive church of St. Dominic, severe and mighty like a fortress.

Fontebranda, St. Dominic's Church, the house of Jacopo Benincasa: the three vertices of a triangle in which one finds the first years of the life of St. Catherine of Siena.

Fontebranda, in the lower point, is the earthly aspect of life. It is the daily fatigue of attending to the material demands of a large family. It is a danger of vain words, of wicked encounters from which to guard oneself.

St. Dominic's Church, up at the top, is the life of the spirit. It is the house of Truth, the blessed place of eucharistic union.

1

And the house, in the middle, is the convergent point of the forces of the other two vertices. It is the place where opposing elements are harmonized in Catherine's incomparable personality.

How many times did Catherine, the twenty-fourth child of Jacopo Benincasa and Monna Lapa, make the jaunt between the house and the fountain? After her refusal of many promising suitors, she remained an object of disdain by the entire family. The maid was dismissed and all of the housework was laid upon Catherine. The work was great, but she was not discouraged. If she refused every proposal of marriage it was because another love, great and immense, had already overwhelmed her entire life. She was only six years old when Jesus appeared to her above the Church of St. Dominic in all the majesty of pontifical vestments accompanied by the apostles Peter, Paul and John. Smiling kindly, Jesus gave her "his eternal blessing."

Biographers later find in this first vision the beginning of Catherine's vocation, the first call to that extraordinary mission which the Lord gave her for the good of the Church. But for her, then, it was simply the beginning of love. She consecrated her entire self and her whole life to the love of Christ by a vow of virginity when she was only seven years old.

Love in the soul colors whatever it sees with

its own light. Love insists upon the presence of the beloved. Catherine seeks him while she does the housework. Love within teaches her the way: Jacopo, the good and pious head of the house, represents the Lord Jesus; Monna Lapa, a little too impetuous it is true, but hardworking and sincere, is the Blessed Mother; her brothers and sisters are the Apostles. Each service done for the members of her family is done for the Lord, for his Blessed Mother, for his saints.

With things arranged like this, Catherine can happily go up and down the street, where the house of her father Jacopo and her Spouse Jesus is located, carrying her load of pure water.

The water bubbles into the jar that Catherine holds under the spout. The large pool under the vault is dark and full of mystery. If a child hangs down from the low wall his mother pulls him back with a fearful shudder. It is frightening to think that a life so new and innocent could be extinguished and swallowed up by that cold, black water.

There is something within us that deserves to die and disappear into the dark water, something that burrows into the most hidden crevices of the soul and undermines the supreme rights of the First Love. Inordinate self-love, "the sensual self-love," is killed and drowned.

"Think, my sweet father," Catherine will write to her first confessor, the Dominican Friar Thomas della Fonte, "that whatever we lack of

3

him, that much we keep for ourselves. That is the very thing we should root out of our will, and kill and drown it, because it deprives us of much rich clothing."[1]

The water, beaded with light, laughs while it gushes from the canal, before stagnating in the black mirror of the pool. There is living water and deadly water, thinks Catherine, and the love of Christ our Savior "takes away the dead water and gives the living water of grace."[2]

> If you ask me, 'How can I have this water?' I will tell you, my daughter, that we can neither have it nor draw it except from the fountain of the First Truth. At this fountain you will find the dignity and beauty of your soul. You will see the Word, the bleeding Lamb, who is given to you as food and at a price, moved only by the fire of his love, and not because of some service he has received from man, who has done nothing but hurt him. I say then that the soul, considering this fountain, hungers and thirsts for virtue, drinking immediately, neither seeing nor loving self. It sees everything in the fountain of God's goodness and because of him loves what he loves, and nothing without him. Now how could the soul that has seen such immense kindness as God, keep from loving? To this the first sweet Truth invited us when

he cried out in the Temple with an ardent heart, saying: 'Whoever is thirsty, come to me and drink, for I am the fountain of living water.' You see, my daughter, that those who thirst are invited. He does not say: who is not thirsty, but: *who is thirsty*. Therefore, ask God that we might carry the jar to an open stream with thirst and a loving will. Let us go to the fountain of the sweet goodness of God, as he said, and in this fountain we will find the knowledge of ourselves and of God. In immersing your jar, you will draw the water of divine grace which is sufficient to give a strong life.[3]

The water's surface reflects the slender figure of a child who searches its depths with her eyes as if to understand the problem worrying her. God is an inexhaustible fountain and there is no one who cannot satisfy his thirst in him. But even in God himself there is a thirst. This was revealed in the most solemn moment of Christ's life.

The first sweet Truth, because of hunger and thirst, had an insatiable desire for our salvation. From the wood of that most holy cross, he cried out: 'I thirst,' as if to say: I have such a tremendous thirst and desire for your salvation that I cannot manifest it with this finite suffering! The suffering of the thirst of holy desire is infinite, and his suffering is finite. As he shows us the thirst that he has for all humanity, we know that he was also afflicted with bodily thirst. O sweet and good Jesus, at the same time you point out the thirst and ask to be given to drink from the soul? When you show us your affection and charity, my Lord... The blood shows us this ineffable love, that because of love you gave the blood and with that love ask us to drink... how fitting that he who loves, be loved. Then the soul gives drink to her Creator when she renders love for love.[4]

The jug is full and Catherine starts for home. It is full, but soon it will be empty: many hands will go and get it. Then Catherine will return anew to Fontebranda to refill it. This is the service which her Spouse asks of her for the moment. The soul cannot fulfill its debt of love to God "by service to him, but by means of one's neighbor."[5]

When the soul examines the many ways in which she can serve God in her neighbor, she finds that "drawing souls out of the hands of the devil pleases our Savior above all other things."[6] Then she will no longer try to put water in an earthen vessel, but make of herself "a vessel" of living water springing up to eternal life.

The Savior is preparing his young bride Catherine for this mission of sharing in his divine thirst for souls, of enabling souls to partake of the living water that springs up from the eternal Fountain. Perhaps, while the weight of the full jug slows her pace up the slope, his discreet and mild voice instructs her interiorly.

> My dearest daughter, I do not want you to act like those who fill the vessel full of water from the fountain, and then drink what they have drawn out, so that it remains empty and they have nothing. But I desire that, filling the vessel of your soul, you do something through love and affection for him whom you love because of love of me, not leaving me, the fountain of living water, but holding the creature that you love for my sake, like a vase in the water. In this way neither you nor the one you love will be empty. You will always be full of divine grace and the most ardent fire of charity.[7]

In the clay jug she carries on her shoulder, Catherine's fingers seem to sense the spiritual substance made worthy to contain such a treasure: "… the angelic nature does not have as much dignity… in the vessel of the soul he has placed his word."[8] If God has done such favors for his creature, "who will be so ignorant and stubborn not to take the vessel of the heart, and lovingly go to the side of Christ crucified, which contains and pours out an abundance of blood?"[9]

Who will be... ? More than one, yes, more than one, how absurd to allow oneself to burn with thirst when the fountain pours forth such abundance. Catherine does not ignore this and encourages her will anew.

> Sweet Jesus asked to drink those he saw did not share in the redemption of his blood. He was given nothing but bitterness to drink. Alas... we continually see that, not just at the time of the cross, but later and now, he continually asks us to drink and he demonstrates a continual thirst. Alas, unfortunate me, I do not think that a creature can give him anything but bitterness and the stench of sins. Therefore, we should raise ourselves up... so that the inebriated soul can desire and love nothing but what God loves.[10]

Catherine will arise at her Bridegroom's command and go far away from her home and Fontebranda. She will faithfully fill the vessel of her soul at the Fountain, and whoever drinks from her will quench their thirst from Christ.

CHAPTER TWO

FIRE AND SPARKS

Catherine enters the house and sets down the jar of water drawn from Fontebranda. Day comes to an end and before long her brothers and the shop boys from her father's dye-shop will stop work. She needs to think about supper and goes to the fireplace.

If the poetry of divine love sings for her in the quiet laughter of the fountain, the crackling and glistening fire draws forth lightning flashes of clear intuition refracting varied and colored images.

How could it be otherwise? Is it not the flame that feeds on inert matter, yet untiringly and obstinately holds to a living image of the destiny of human life? The flame purifies: assimilating what it attacks. Is this not an obvious image of divine charity?

The fire sleeps for now under the ashes, like grace in a distracted soul. At the fireside, Catherine shakes the embers, making the ashes fall off, and skillfully places the wood in a pile between the andirons.

A little flame frees itself from the embers, licking the first logs. The wood covered with smooth bark resists it. The little flame comes and goes somewhat timidly, weak and uncertain. A log begins to groan, then several flames spring out, lively aggressive lights: all burn the stack in the chimney.

Catherine contemplates the flame flickering in the fireplace. She contemplates the invisible flame of charity. What feeds this spiritual fire? Truth, that fundamental truth which is the source and center of all human history: love that creates, love that redeems. The eye of the intellect needs to look upward,

> to look at the ineffable eye of divine charity, with which God watched, and still looks after, his creature before he created us. Since he saw himself immensely loving, he created us out of love, and wanted us to enjoy and share in the good that he had in himself, but the sin of Adam did not fulfill his desire. Impelled by the fire of divine charity, God sent the sweet incarnate word of his Son. The Son hurries and gives himself to the disgrace of the cross... Love can impose neither laws nor measure.[1]
>
> [One should never cease] putting the wood of self-knowledge on the fire of holy desire. These are the logs that nourish the fire of divine charity... uniting

the soul with its neighbor. The more one
gives fuel to the fire (that is, the word of
self-knowledge) so much more increases
the warmth of love for Christ and one's
neighbor.[2]

Now that the flame has conquered, the black
logs slowly become burning embers. The material
that shortly before resisted the fire has now itself
become fire. It was enough for Catherine to ex-
pose the wood to the flames, leaving it to be penetrated by the fire.

What will help a person bring his or her in-
dependent, not to say rebellious, will and keep it
in the red-hot field of divine action?

One cannot be united to another person
except by bonds, nor can he become
one thing with the fire if he does not
throw himself in it, so that nothing remains outside. This is that bond of love
with which the soul is united to Christ. O
how great is that sweet bond which
united the Son of God to the holy wood
of the cross! The human person finds
himself in the fire when he is bound by
this chain.[3]

It is no longer a dead log that Catherine sees
burning on the hearth, but the human person with
the clear knowledge of self and the goodness of
God manifested in the mystery of the Passion of

the Son of God. Thus, the burden of poverty, of sin, of the ingratitude which is added to one's life history, becomes the tinder for the fire of love in Christ's redemptive action, love and blood.

> Make the fire of divine charity in the soul like the material fire that warms and illumines and converts things into itself. O sweet fire that heats and drives out all coldness of vice and sin and self-love! This heat warms and ignites this dry wood of our will. It ignites and spreads the sweet and loving desires, loving what God loves and hating what God hates. I tell you that as the soul sees itself to be loved so immensely and given the same bleeding lamb on the wood of the most holy cross, I say that the fire enlightens and she does not fall into darkness. In this way, the soul is illuminated by this venerable fire, completely extending and enlarging the understanding. And then the one who has experienced and received the light, discerns and sees what is God's will, and desires to follow only the path of Christ crucified.[4]

No one can escape that blazing fire of love. "They are like the burning coal that no one can put out once it is consumed in the furnace because it has itself been turned into fire."[5]

The flames flare up from the burning woodpile on the hearth. They disappear, darting up the black throat of the chimney which tapers off at the top towards the pure and free air. So too, the human person conquering the burden of egoism runs freely along the way of his Master.

> When the understanding has received the light of the fire... it becomes one thing with it, and so the memory becomes one thing with Christ crucified, whom one cannot believe nor enjoy nor think of, if not to enjoy what he loves. He sees that ineffable love which he has for all humanity, and immediately commits it to memory and becomes a lover of God and neighbor. He does not look at the usefulness that he draws from him, only because he sees above all that God loves his creature, delighting himself to love what the three powers of the soul unite in this fire: the memory, to recall the benefits of God; the understanding, to comprehend his goodness and will...; the will opens out to love so that he can have no other love, desiring nothing but him. All of her actions are directed towards him. She always thinks of doing what pleases her creator... This is the way of Christ crucified.[6]

"God gave us the Word, his only-begotten Son, and the Word gave us the blood: giving up his life he returned us to grace with such a fire of love."[7]

> "There is no blood without fire, nor fire without blood."[8] This sweet fire has not ended nor will it ever end. If his affection for us would come to an end, we would cease, for the being that he gave us would end. Only the fire of love moves him to draw us to himself.[9]

The burning logs explode and the swarming sparks escape upwards. The momentary flash vanishes even before reaching the mantle of the chimney. It seems to Catherine that the "mouth of truth" says to her: I am the fire, and you are the sparks.

It is true, Catherine thinks. What is the little flame of our charity in comparison with the immense furnace of divine charity? It is something like the enormous disproportion of the smallness of our being before "He Who Is." But still, this being of ours is something that comes from him and participates in his beauty and goodness.

> O ineffable, delightful charity, you speak the truth well: it is good for us to be the sparks, since you want us to be humble. Just as the spark receives its being from the fire, so we acknowledge being from our first principle, since you said, 'I am fire and you are sparks.'[10]

14

The soul finds true humility in charity, if it acts like the spark that first goes up and then comes back down. The first movement of our holy desire is in the knowledge of God and his honor. Then, having risen, we now descend to know our misery and negligence. O sleeper, awake! Thus we will be humble, finding ourselves in the abyss of his charity. O sweet mother of charity, there is nothing so hard, or so dormant that it will not awaken or melt with such a fire of charity.[11]

When the soul considers and sees the great excellence and strength of the fire of the Holy Spirit within herself, she is inebriated, and knowing her creator's love she completely surrenders herself. Living, she is dead and feels within herself neither love nor pleasure for creatures, since the memory is already filled with the affection of her creator. The understanding seeks neither to understand nor see any created thing separate from God. It understands and sees herself only as non-being, and the goodness of God within herself. She sees that infinite goodness wants nothing but her good. Then her love towards God has become perfect; since she has nothing within herself, she cannot hold to the rapid race of desire, but runs without any weight or chain.[12]

The soul hurled upon the way of divine love is enabled to proceed inadvertently from contemplation to ecstasy. It happens this way to Catherine. Her sister-in-law Lisa finds her one day stretched out upon the burning embers, insensible. After the first fearful moment, joy wells up in Lisa at seeing that the fire has respected Catherine, leaving her clothing and body intact. It even cooks the roast that the saint had intended to turn; or better, that she turned while intent upon her thoughts when the ecstasy took away her "understanding of created things."

Brother Fire would have been ashamed to harm someone who looked at him with such a loving mind. He also treated St. Francis of Assisi well, who called him "handsome and robust and strong," praising God for the light of the flame that conquers the darkness of night. But Catherine contemplates the divine fire of eternal Love.

"The Love of the Holy Spirit is this fire."[13]

CHAPTER THREE

THE POT ON THE FIRE

Anyone who thinks Catherine was continually absorbed in ecstasies and unaware of the things of daily life is a long way from understanding her soul. Her insensibility during an ecstasy was completely from the physical viewpoint; her soul always retained the ability of communicating in words. This is different from other types of ecstasies. Thus, she was able to dictate some letters and *The Dialogue* while "in abstraction." Anyway, ecstasy was not the ordinary condition in her life. It would be completely off-track to imagine her incapable of observing life in its various aspects and gathering humorous tidbits. Life is not a farce, it is real. The serious and witty moments are constantly found shoulder to shoulder and a careful and intelligent observer cannot help but realize this. Besides, Catherine is Italian and Tuscan!

How many different and various things move about in the Benincasa environment! Catherine watches and observes; sometimes she is saddened and sometimes she smiles. Perhaps even while an image is still broadening her lips in a smile, her eyes are pensive because her mind has just grasped a spiritual reality.

Monna Lapa arrives, totally preoccupied and agitated because she cannot find the key to her cabinet. She had it in her hand a short while ago, and now when she needs it, she cannot find it. Perhaps she is a little embarrassed to ask Catherine because the reason for locking things up is precisely a precaution against Catherine, to keep her from giving all of the family's things to the poor. Naturally, it was Jacopo's fault for giving her permission to give alms whenever she wanted. But there is a limit to everything, at least there ought to be…

"What are you looking for, Mama?"

"My key… "

"It's there, on the bench!"

Catherine smiles faintly at Lapa's joyful embarrassment. Already her thoughts fly to the treasure, the great, immensely rich treasure which is reserved for us in the kingdom of Heaven: the only one that is worth guarding. Is that treasure locked up? Is there a key to open it? Oh, yes: the key is obedience. Adam did not want to have anything to do with it and threw it away — not like Monna Lapa who had only forgotten hers. He threw it in the mire and no one could open the treasure anymore; first, because the key was hidden in the mud, and then because it seemed useless.

18

He smashed it with the hammer of pride
and let it get rusty with selfishness. Not
until the Word my only-begotten Son
came was this key of obedience picked
up again. He purified it in the fire of divine charity after he had picked it out of
the mire and washed it with his blood.
With the knife of justice he straightened
it out and on the anvil of his body he
hammered out your iniquities.[1]

This "mended" key is given to each person
at baptism, "so each of you individually has it, the
very Word's key." A person who wants to enter
needs to go "by the light of faith and with the
hand of love to open heaven's gate with this key."

What if a person breaks the key as Adam
did? Free will, the instrument that broke it, will be
the instrument to repair it. Confession restores
what had been given in baptism. But it is necessary to take care of it, not to lose it.

Tie this key tightly with the cord of lowliness and contempt for yourself and the
world. Attach it to desire to please me
your Creator. You ought to make yourself a belt of this desire, so that you will
not lose the key.

Know, my daughter, that many people
have taken hold of the key of obedience
when they have seen by the light of faith
that in no other way can they escape

eternal damnation. But they hold it in their hand without tying it with this cord or fastening it to this belt. In other words, they do not clothe themselves perfectly in the desire to please me but are only interested in pleasing themselves. They have not tied on the cord of lowliness by desiring to be considered lowly; rather, they have found their pleasure in being praised by others. They are likely to lose the key… [loosening] the grip of their desire… This is a loss that can be recovered, if they are willing, so long as they are alive. But if they are not willing, they will never find it. [2]

Jacopo, seated at his desk and immersed in business accounts, does not pay much attention to the worries of his wife. It is always this way with Lapa: agitated, excited… and that blessed daughter Catherine, who has suffered many of her mother's battles, always ends by calming her down.

The door opens. A merchant who borrowed money some time ago comes to return it. Jacopo is not the type to lend with interest. He lends gladly as a favor to a colleague who finds himself in need. God looks after him! The friend had to insist he make a note for the loan, although his word would have been enough for Jacopo. Well then, here is the note. He can repay it only in installments.

The merchant is fortunate to have found such a kind creditor. He is fortunate also in the deal they made to repay the pledged sum. It usually does not happen like this, and bad debtors of hardhearted lenders end up in prison.

Humanity was in these straits after Adam's sin. It had a huge debt that it would never have been able to pay, but found someone to pay it, and at what a price! "Not in gold nor with the sweetness of love, but with blood."

> Break open your hearts and souls with love. Rise up eagerly to serve and fear the sweet and good Jesus. Consider how he drew us out from prison and slavery to the devil who possessed us as his own. He made a guarantee and payment, and tore up the note of obligation. When did he make the guarantee? When he became a servant taking on our humanity.

> Alas, it was not enough unless he paid our debt for us. And when did he pay it? On the wood of the most holy cross, giving his life to obtain the life of grace for us that we had lost. O inestimable and sweetest charity! You have destroyed the note that was between humanity and the devil, tearing it up on the wood of the most holy cross. The note was paid by none other than the lamb. He is that immaculate lamb who wrote us into his very being. But he tore up this note. Therefore, we encourage our souls since we are inscribed there and the note is

destroyed. We can no longer be domi-
nated by the adversary and our contrary
selves.[3]

How sad it is to think that, after such a benefit, evil and ungrateful people again "make new
debt notes with the devil every day."[4] Why, if not
out of self-love, the cause of every sin? Those
who truly love God "died because they no longer
thought of themselves."[5]

Yet, her father Jacob, or any owner of a
business, knows that one no longer has the money
at one's disposal that has been lent out.

The apprentices come and go with heavy
bales of cloth. This one is "dead." He does nothing but complain that the weight is too heavy and
sits down every two minutes, huffing and puffing
under the load. That other one, agile and vigorous, puts his cargo on his shoulder and walks
quickly. This way is good, "carry, carry, and make
your shoulder a carrier." Catherine knows what it
means to carry a burden. She has never hesitated
to go all the way up to the attic with a sack of
grain on her slender, but strong, shoulders. Physical toil then, is not such a great problem. The
suffering of the heart is much more difficult.

Let us carry, let us carry on... because
the more pain we bear down here for
Christ crucified, the more glory we will
receive. No suffering will be so rewarded
as weariness of heart and mental suffer-

ing, because they are the greatest suf-
ferings there are and so are worthy of
greater fruit.[6]

But is not a person ridiculous who "remains
on earth with perverse indignation,"[7] similar to a
naughty boy who does not want to listen to reason?

The gurgling of the pot of boiling bean soup
recalls Catherine's attention to the fireplace. There
is something else interesting in her kitchen: the
aroma attracts the flies, but the heat of the fire
repels them. Catherine watches their maneuvers.
They remain a little while suspended in air buzz-
ing with invisible wings, waiting the most oppor-
tune moment for the attack; then leave quickly.
They are on the offensive returning soon with a
quick turn.

Catherine amuses herself by watching how
each attack unfailingly changes into a retreat. Not
because she is at enmity with the flies because
they are flies, but because their defeat brings to
her mind another one. The attack that the de-
mons have the habit of raising against her every
time she enters her cell, "like a swarm of bother-
some flies." Toward the end of her life, when she
dictates her *Dialogue*, the image of the flies around
the pot of soup has lost nothing of its honest hu-
mor.

It is indeed true that the devil never sleeps
but teaches you, if you are careless, to

23

sleep when it is profitable to him. But his watching cannot hurt these [that is, those who, united to God by full conformity of their will with the divine will, are concerned neither with consolations nor tribulations]... for he cannot stand the heat of their charity, nor the fragrance of their soul's union with me, the sea of peace. No, the soul cannot be tricked so long as she remains united with me. So the devil flees like a fly from a boiling caldron, because he is afraid of the fire. If the soul were lukewarm he would enter fearlessly though often enough he perishes there when he finds it hotter than he had imagined.[8]

This is exactly what happened to the devil-fly when he thought he could conquer Catherine. Seeing her so young, he had judged her to be a beginner in the spiritual life; but her prompt and sure response left him confused.

I chose suffering for my joy. It is not difficult for me to bear these and other persecutions in the name of the Savior as long as it shall please his Majesty. I even enjoy them.[9]

Every defeat of Satan is a victory for God. Therefore, the smile at the flies brushed away from the pot lingers on Catherine's pensive face.

CHAPTER FOUR

THE TABLE AND THE EAGLE

When the Benincasa family is gathered around the dinner table neither quantity nor variety is lacking among the table companions.

There is Jacopo the excellent *paterfamilias*. There is Lapa, mother of 25 children and as active and industrious as a bee.[1] She is more inclined to housework and the affairs of her family than the things of the spirit. She will never be able to understand her spiritual daughter. There are Catherine's brothers and sisters, not all present because some are married and others elsewhere due to their trades. However, their empty places are gradually filled by a new generation of little Benincasas, the children of Bartholomew Benincasa and Lisa Colombini.

Of all the members of the family, perhaps Lisa is the one closest in spirit to Catherine, who calls her "sister-in-law according to the flesh, sister in Jesus Christ."

If Catherine sits at table with her family she does so out of obedience to an explicit command of her Spouse and Lord. She endured years of persecution by her family when they tried to break her determined will to consecrate herself completely to the service of God. She learned how to find "the desert within the walls of her own house and solitude in the midst of people"[2] and in the silence of her little room. After years of very severe ascetical discipline, when Christ visited her to instruct her about the Kingdom of God, reveal divine secrets to her, and recite the Psalms of the Liturgy of the Hours with her, our Lord said, "Go! It is dinner time and your family want to go to table. Go, be with them and then return to me."

Obedience is not without difficulty or tears. "Why, sweetest Spouse, do you send me away? … What does eating matter to me?… Does man live on bread alone?"

But the Lord reassures her by explaining that he would have her fulfill both of the commandments that summarize the Law of God. It does not take her away, but enables her to be even more intimately united to him in charity. "Remain calm, my sweetest daughter. You know that there are two precepts of love. I want you to fulfill these two commandments. In fact, you must walk, not with one, but two feet, and with two wings fly to heaven."[3]

When she was only a child, Catherine would mortify herself by secretly passing her portion of meat to the dog under the table. Now, however, it is no longer necessary to conceal her abstinence. Everyone knows now that her stomach, unaccustomed to food, cannot tolerate the smallest amount, even the size of a nut! Her graceful appearance is such that no one even thinks of teasing her.

Naturally, it was not always like this. There was a time when the wonder of living only on the Eucharist caused ceaseless murmuring and malicious judgments about her. It was so great that Catherine begged her Spouse to take from her that privilege which had become a stumbling block for some. She apologized with such humility as to subdue the most spiteful murmurers.

If, then, Catherine comes to sit with her family at table, it is obvious that she comes not to receive but to give. She brings to the assembled family the happiness of a presence overflowing with the presence of God. It is that "serene tranquillity within the soul, of a will in tune with and subject to reason, that is scandalized by nothing."[4] It is the fruit of a loving affection that prays continually in the presence of God. Did not the Lord send her out to practice charity towards her relatives? Charity grieves with one who is sad and rejoices with one who rejoices. It takes an interest in the daily events of whoever begins the evening conversation. It encourages a good thought and controls a harsh judgment. Charity is also alert to all the needs of those who are seated at table, mindful of who lacks wine or bread, and concerned that the little girl asleep with her head on her arm does not end up on the floor.

Material food is of no interest to Catherine. She finds the spiritual food that the Master tasted near Jacob's well when he opened the mind of the Samaritan woman to the mysteries of the Kingdom of God. "My food is to do the will of him who sent me, and to accomplish his work."[5] The Son of God was truly hungry for food to such an extent as to die. His hunger was conceived in his love and knowledge of the Father.

> It is good that this sweet Word became like an eagle that follows the path of the sun and always sees from on high the food he wants to seize. He sees it down on the ground, comes and takes it, and then eats it up above. In this way, our eagle, sweet Jesus, considers the eternal will of God in the sun and there he sees the offense and rebellion of the creature he made. Thus in the earth of the creature which is found in the loftiness of the Father, he saw the food that he should take. His food is of this miserable earth which has offended and rebelled against God by wretched disobedience. By his obedience he takes the willingness to accomplish in man the truth of the Father, restores grace and draws him from the slavery of the devil. That sla-

very is eternal death. And he obliges him
to the service of his Creator. Since he
has seen and taken the food that the
Father had given him to eat, he sees that
down on the earth he cannot eat... and
is therefore raised up as a victim on the
height of the most holy cross, and there
he eats with intense and indescribable
desire.[6]

Perhaps Catherine's eyes wander across the
Sienese sky to discover an image. Perhaps she
has sometimes seen the hunter falcon soar and
disappear in the sun. Then in an instant it reap-
pears, pouncing upon its victim, seizing and carrying it off on high.

"And the soul cries out, saying, 'O Sweet
God, what do you love most?' Our gentle God
responds, 'Look within yourself and you will find
what I love.'"[7] So too, the soul ascends on high
and looks at the earth, and finding the inexpress-
ible mystery of the incarnate Word dead because
of love, receives from him that hunger for souls
that is satiated upon the cross.

Like the eagle who follows the course of
the sun and goes up high and then looks
at the earth, taking food which nourishes
it, eating it in the air; so too, is the creature who gazes above where the sun of
divine love is and then gazes toward the
earth, that is, towards the humanity of

the incarnate Word of the Son of God. Looking at that Word and humanity drawn forth from the sweet womb of Mary, she sees food on this table and eats it, not only in the earth of Christ's humanity, which she is near, but rising on high with food in her mouth. Once raised above she enters into the soul of the Son of God which is consumed and burning with love. That tender love finds that it is one fire that issues from the power of the Father which gave us the wisdom of his Son and the courage of the fire of the Holy Spirit...[8]

A person finds divine charity in the soul of Christ crucified and in this abyss becomes "an eater and taster of souls." In this tasting and eating of souls the person is satiated by the true food that is Christ, because charity is put into practice and grows by working for one's neighbor.

O sweet Lamb roasted by the fire of divine charity on the stake of the cross! O most delightful food, full of joy, happiness and consolation. There is nothing lacking in you, because for the soul that truly serves you, you become her table, food and waiter. We see well that the Father is the table and bed where the soul can rest. We see the Word, his only Son who is given to you as food, with so much fire of love. Who brings it to you?

The waiter is the Holy Spirit. Because of the great love he has for us, he is not satisfied that we are served by others, but he himself wants to be the waiter. Inflame, therefore, inflame the fire of holy desire...[9]

Those who think they can satisfy their spiritual hunger by any other food are foolish. The Lord told Catherine:

Without me they could never be satisfied even if they possessed the whole world. This is because created things are less than the human person. They were made for you, not you for them, and so they can never satisfy you. Only I can satisfy you. These wretched souls, then, caught in such blindness, are forever toiling but never satisfied.[10]

The soul is made to enjoy the angelic food of the desire of God, and this compels it to raise itself above the baseness of the passions. This height is the greatest of the exercises of heroic virtue "with the pains of anguish, scorn and harsh reproaches for the sake of Christ crucified."[11] It is being above in the bosom of the Father, where desire, painful in the time of testing, will become blessed in its full satisfaction.

Just souls, says the Lord,

...desire me forever, and forever they possess me, so their desire is not in vain.

31

They are hungry and satisfied, satisfied yet hungry — but they are far from bored with satiety and pained in their hunger... That soul finds joy in me and in all these souls and blessed spirits, seeing and tasting in them the sweetness of my love. Their desires are a continual cry to me for the salvation of others...[12]

A brief, almost repressed, wail brings Catherine back to earth. Her friend, the accomplice of her first fasts, stares at her for a while with imploring eyes. Catherine smiles. That rascal is not content with the crumbs that fall from the table like the puppies of Canaan.

In this life [we] can have nothing but the crumbs that fall from the dinner table as in Canaan. The crumbs are the grace that we receive from the Lord's table. But when we shall be in everlasting life where we will taste God and see him face to face, then we will have the food of the table.[13]

At that time the entire family of the elect will be happily gathered around the table of the eternal Father. Now is the time for labor and conquest. It is the time to eat and taste souls at the table of the cross.

"Well then, be brave, without any servile fear!"[14]

CHAPTER FIVE

HARD BREAD AND MILK

Catherine's gaze seeks out and rests upon the smallest of the entire family seated at table. Her affection for them is immeasurable. The grace that gives her a sensitivity for spiritual reality makes her head turn from the stench of those who live in sin, and enjoy the perfume of innocence and grace of pure souls.

How swiftly the little children of yesterday become teenagers and adults! They present themselves as soon as possible at the common table, settling on the highest stool. They make it a point of honor to eat what the adults eat, even if it costs more work.

Catherine likes this vitality of the children who strive to become "mature adults." It will not be a devout memory alone that heightens the tone of her vehement reproach of Blessed Raymond when he takes shelter in Genoa, fearing pirates and not concluding his mission for the King of France.

I write to you with desire to see you this very day get rid of your childhood and be a fearless man. Leave your childhood and be a brave man. Quit tasting milk and become an eater of bread. The child who is nourished by milk is not suitable for battle but delights only in wanting to play with his peers. However, when he becomes a man he gets rid of self-love. He eats bread with the mouth of holy desire, crushing it with the teeth of hate and of love in such a way that the harder and moldier it is, the more he enjoys it. O how blessed is that soul considered when one sees the gums bleeding!... These have refused the milk. The marks of Christ's wounds shine in them as they follow his sweet doctrine... In bitterness, they taste a great sweetness...

God... wanted you to know your own imperfection. He showed you that you are still a child instead of a man feeding himself with bread. If he had seen that you had teeth fit for that, he would not have given you... You were not yet worthy to be in his battlefield, but you were driven back like a child. You willingly fled and rejoiced... Pull out your baby teeth and try to cut strong teeth of hatred and love![1]

With their young and healthy teeth, the children happily devour the pieces cut from the large loaf of brown bread. Catherine herself had kneaded and baked the loaf of bread some four or five days ago. One cannot bake bread every day, so each time enough is made for the entire week. When it is very hard she dips it in water, or even better in wine, so it becomes tastier than when the same bread was fresh. Children know this! The same is true on a spiritual level.

> They are eaters of moldy, but not dry bread. Their teeth could not crush the dry bread very well, except with great fatigue and little results. Therefore, they soak it in the blood of Christ crucified in the fountain of his side. As if intoxicated with love, they run to put the moldy bread of many trials into this precious blood.[2]

It is proper to the strong and brave soul, the soul who is master of self, to turn away from the milk of sensible consolations and instead enjoy the mysterious sweetness of hard and moldy bread, moistened in the blood of Christ. In this way it courageously embraces trials out of love for him. "Bitterness seems like milk," Catherine counsels Fra Francesco Tebaldi, a Cistercian on the Island of Gorgona, "and the milk of one's own consolations seems bitter because of the holy hatred of self."[3]

The same language cannot be used with everyone. Only one who lacks the virtue of discretion or prudence — a typically catherinian value — can pretend that all follow the same way and can be scandalized if they do not keep to the way. Bearded and wrinkled old men can still be less than novices in the life of the spirit. For that reason, on Holy Thursday Catherine takes pen in hand to invite some prisoners in Siena to celebrate Easter worthily. She takes her gaze from the children who eat the food of adults at the common table, and contemplates the smallest one who calmly nurses at its mother's breast.

There is an analogy, which does not escape Catherine, between this new life that is growing in its own autonomy and self-consciousness while resting in complete abandonment upon the breast that conceived and nourishes it, and our relationship as creatures with our Creator-God. Her penetrating spirit perceives every aspect. God is the source of every life. Divine life does not flow within us except by means of the humanity of Christ. Therefore, he becomes the source from which we draw, moved directly by the desire that he himself inflames within us.

> Just as the infant when quieted rests on its mother's breast, takes her nipple and drinks her milk through her flesh; this is how the soul rests on the breast of my divine charity and takes into the mouth of her holy desire the flesh of Christ crucified. In other words, she follows his

teaching and his footsteps, because she
has learned… that she could not follow
after me, the Father. For no pain can
befall me, the eternal Father, but it can
befall my beloved Son… [The soul] drinks
in the milk of virtue… and sweetness.[4]

Here we find both analogy and antithesis
because that confident abandon which is purely
instinctive in the baby, in the spiritual person is
the acquisition and fruit of a severe asceticism.
The soul needs not only to *endure* trials patiently,
but to *desire* them cheerfully, in order to taste the
milk of peace in union with God.

Catherine insists upon this image of the baby
fed at its mother's breast in order to stimulate the
soul to devote itself to this endeavor of union with
the divine will. Today the little Benincasa is not
well and needs to take some medicine. But who
could persuade the infant to swallow and digest a
prepared bitter medicine? The mother knows what
to do. This time, as at other times, she takes the
medicine herself and the baby receives it without
knowing it with the sweet maternal milk.

Our Savior, thinks Catherine, does the same
with us. He took to himself all the bitterness of the
Passion. He gave us the fruit through his holy
Blood. She begins her letter,

In the name of Jesus Christ crucified and
sweet Mary.

Dearest children in sweet Christ Jesus, I Catherine… write you in his precious blood, with desire to see you bathed with holy desire in the blood of Christ crucified… The blood of Christ reveals our iniquities and the infinite mercy and charity of God…

The human person was infirm and feeble, rebelling against his Creator. He could not take the bitter medicine that accompanied the sin committed. It was necessary, therefore, that God gave us the Lord, his only-begotten Son… He came as a doctor…

He took on our infirmities. He took on our mortal flesh and mortality. He punished our defects in that flesh of his most sweet body. He was like the wet-nurse who nourishes the infant. She takes the medicine for the baby when it is sick, because the infant is small and weak and unable to take the bitterness. It feeds on nothing but milk. O sweetest love, Jesus, you are the wet-nurse who took the bitter medicine, bearing pain, disgrace, torture, insult… O priceless love, it is not enough that you pray for those who crucify you, but you excuse them… O patience that exceeds every patience! Who being struck, beaten, mocked, and killed, ever pardons and prays for those who offend him? You alone are he, my Lord. It is wonderful, therefore, that you took the bitter medicine for us, weak and infirm infants. You give us life with your death and sweetness through your bitterness. You hold us at the breast like a wet-nurse and give us the milk of divine grace. You removed the bitterness and so we receive sanctity. Thus, you see how he was infirm for us.[5]

This illustration of the Redeemer sharing in our infirmities, tender as a mother with her sick baby, evokes other images of families, mothers, wives, and sisters, in the spirits of the poor prisoners who are separated from all affection! The ardent eloquence that penetrates that gentle image, transporting it to Calvary in the harsh reality of the Passion, "mockery, disgrace… thirst without comfort… the greatest reproach," enables each one to see something of his own present reality. How could it leave their hearts cold?

So I tell you… bathe yourselves in the blood of Christ, because we can share in his grace in no other way… nor be able to carry patiently your crosses. In the remembrance of the blood every bitterness becomes sweet and every heavy burden, light.[6]

As the hard bread in wine, as the medicine in the mother's milk, so too, the blood like the milk is given out of love. There is nothing sweeter than love.

Chapter Six

MATERIAL FOR THE FLAME

The large room in which the numerous and noisy Benincasa family gathers is deserted. By ones, twos and threes, the young and old left in a little circle of candlelight. The candles were lit from the oil lamp that burns on the table. The atmosphere, full of silence and shadow, has acquired unreal proportions extending beyond the limits of the almost invisible walls.

Catherine has covered the embers with ashes. The dog has gone to stretch out next to the hearth to enjoy the fading warmth. It appears to be sleeping, but at the least suspicious sound it raises its eyes and growls dully between its teeth. The rhythm of footsteps on the cobblestones makes it leap up on all four paws and run to the street door, straining and pulsating with its muzzle flattened against an opening in the shutters.

This is how our conscience should be: always on guard. It should be prepared for all the surprises of an enemy that does not sleep. It is prepared to rebuke him before he has acquired

41

anything! "A dog stationed at the gate barks when it sees enemies, and by its barking wakes up… the guard of reason."[1]

The "dog of conscience" is fed so that it will be strong and alert. If the dog does not eat it will become weak and not bark. "The dog of his conscience is so weakened for want of feeding that it cannot bark. The food that must be given to this dog is the blood of the Lamb… , my Son. For if the memory, as the vessel of the soul, is filled with the blood, conscience will be nourished by it. In other words, the remembrance of the blood sets the soul afire with hatred of sin and love for virtue."[2]

Catherine arranges the table so that it will be ready for breakfast the following day. She will have already had her one meal of the day before the family returns to gather around the large table. As with her abstinence from material food, she receives harsh criticism also for her desire for the eucharistic food. Who would consider themselves bold enough to receive the Body of the Lord everyday? Once she was asked her reason for wanting to receive communion everyday, something which St. Augustine neither praised nor blamed. "Does it not, therefore, seem great boldness to communicate everyday?" She replied, "I would not be happy to be good only once a year or once a month or week. On the contrary, it is a great joy and consolation to be good everyday. St. Augustine says that it does not offend to be very good."

The warfare was not limited to criticism. How many times her hunger for the Eucharist was denied! The Lord allowed this only to increase the fire of desire within her.

> Sometimes, to intensify her hunger and holy desire, I will let her desire them when she cannot have them. Because she cannot have them her hunger grows, and with her hunger her self-knowledge grows because in her humility she considers herself unworthy. Then I make her worthy and often I provide this sacrament in different ways.[3]

Catherine knows this well. Many times God provides her with those things which people deny her. After these gratuitous and miraculous interventions of his omnipotence, "if she had the tiniest bit of faith and love before, it now grew to overflowing fullness with such great longing that it seemed as if life wanted to leave her body."[4]

While she is completing the last duties of the day, Catherine has already returned "by desire to the table of the Lamb" who repeats within her heart: "I am the table and the food."[5]

> Every other table is without fruit, but this one has the perfect life-giving fruit. This is a pierced table full of veins that pro-

duce blood. A canal runs between them and throws out blood and water mixed with fire. The secret of his heart is manifested to one who gazes upon this canal. This blood is a wine which intoxicates the soul. The more one drinks of it the more one wants it and is never satisfied because the blood and flesh are united with the infinite God.[6]

Perfect in itself and inexhaustible, the eucharistic table varies in its fruits as the dispositions of souls vary.

If you had a burning lamp and all the world came to you for light, the light of your lamp would not be diminished by sharing it, yet each person who shared it would have the whole light. True, each one's light would be more or less intense depending on what sort of material each brought to receive the fire... Imagine that many people brought candles, and one person's candle weighed one ounce, another's two or six, someone else's a pound, and yet another's more than that, and they all came to your lamp to light their candles. Each candle, the smallest as well as the largest, would have the whole light with all its heat and color and brightness. Still, you would think that the person who carried the one-ounce

44

candle would have less than the one whose candle weighed a pound. Well, this is how it goes with those who receive this sacrament. Each one of you brings your own candle, that is, the holy desire with which you receive and eat this sacrament.[7]

Everything is in order and Catherine, as the others earlier, lights a candle from the lantern to brighten the way to her small room. The little flame wavers at each step. It flickers with every gust of air as if it were going out, but glowingly revives when her hand shields it. A little lake of melted wax has formed around the wick and the wax rises up the wick to feed the flame. Thus, the candle slowly consumes itself without leaving a trace, without a residue. The wax is made to burn as the soul is made to love.

"It is I," says the Lord to Catherine, "who have given you the candle with which you can receive this light and nourish it within yourself. And your candle is love, because it is for love that I created you, so without love you cannot have life."

But wax, which by nature is meant to be transformed into a flame, would not be able to burn without a wick. What is the wick of the soul?

Your being was given to you for love,
and in holy baptism... you were made

ready to share this light. There is no other way you could come to share it. Indeed, you would be like a candle that has no wick, and therefore can neither burn nor even receive the light. So if you would bear this light, you must receive the wick that is faith. And to this grace that you receive in baptism you must join your own soul's love. For I created your soul with a capacity for loving — so much so that you cannot live without love. Indeed, love is your food.

Once the soul is so prepared, where is she to be lighted? At the flame of my divine charity... And she will take fire more or less intensely depending on the material she brings to this flame.

Yes, faith makes supernatural love possible. But when sin has destroyed grace, how can the soul receive "this sweet sacrament"?

She is like a candle that has been doused with water and only hisses when it is brought near the fire. The flame no more than touches it, but it goes out and nothing remains but smoke... She will have gained nothing from this sacrament but the hissing of remorse...[8]

Catherine keeps vigil in her cell while everyone else in the house sleeps. She remains awake, not only to enjoy uninterrupted intimacy with Christ, her Spouse; not only to grow in her desire for God — "holy desire prays continually" in her soul because "every time is the time for him, and every place is the place for him"[9] — but to "extend sweet and loving desires with an enkindled and burning heart" for the honor of God and the salvation of neighbor without ever losing sight of Christ crucified and his infinite desire for souls.[10]

> Regarding this holy desire, according to the divine grace given to me — since I am nothing of myself, but only God is He who is — so as God has wounded the soul, I dare to say with Christ: "With desire I have desired that we celebrate the Passover before we die." This will be our sweet and holy Pasch of which David spoke in the Psalter: "Taste and see." But it does not seem that we can see God unless we first celebrate and taste this holy Passover. I say savor it through love of his priceless affection of charity, knowing and tasting the goodness of God that wants nothing but our good... O inestimable affection and charity. To manifest this red-hot desire you ran like someone drunk and blind to the disgrace of the cross.[11]

Yes, Christ crucified has wounded the soul of his bride. Or rather, he has fashioned it to the

likeness of his own soul. The soul is fuel for love.
Just as it can burn as it draws near the fire of
divine charity, so too it can receive and retain its
imprint "as a figure stamped on wax."[12] This is
the proper effect of eucharistic communion: the
divine presence leaves the imprint of its divine
grace in the soul, "just as a seal that is pressed
into warm wax leaves its imprint when it is lifted
off."[13] This imprint is the strength of the Father
and the warmth of the Holy Spirit, but above all,
the wisdom of the Son, eternal Truth, that illu-
mines the soul with his doctrine.

It is for this reason that Catherine continues
her vigil: to draw souls away from the hands of
the enemy, to pull them from the death-dealing
water that does not let the flame of love burn and
to enable souls to become docile material for the
divine seal.

> She now stretched out her prayer, like a
> starving person, to the whole world...
> She cried out: "Have mercy, eternal God,
> on your little sheep, good shepherd that
> you are! Do not delay with your mercy
> for the world, for already it almost seems
> that they can no longer survive. Every-
> one seems bereft of any unity of charity
> with you, eternal Truth, or even with
> each other: I mean, whatever love they
> have for each other has no grounding in
> you." [Then God, like one drunk for our

good,] responded by igniting an ever greater love and suffering within her.[14]

Catherine keeps vigil like this for a long time until the tolling of the bell at St. Dominic's calls the friars to the midnight prayers of Matins. Only then, when she is certain that praise and supplication will continue to ascend to God from the choir of her brothers in the large church that dominates the Camporegio hill, will she allow herself to go to sleep with a final desire to be the light of the "first sweet Truth." *Illumina oculos meos, ne unquam obdormiam in morte.* [Enlighten my eyes, that they may not sleep in death.]

Then, when the sky begins to melt in the first rays of the new day, Catherine rises from sleep and silently leaves the house. She ascends the steep path to St. Dominic's Church. Her heart is yearning with desire and bowed with humility. Her Spouse will be awaiting her there, desirous of her no less than she is of him.

She will see and taste "the depth of the Trinity, wholly God, wholly human, hidden and veiled under the whiteness"[15] of the eucharistic bread.

He will give a new flame to her candle and imprint upon it anew the seal of his divine face.

CHAPTER SEVEN

THE CELL

There is a small room in the Benincasa house in Siena. That dark room is one of those places one enters with a feeling of fearful respect for holy places. It is a narrow space closed between low walls with a tiny window. On the pavement beneath the window is an iron grating protecting the stone which served as a pillow for Catherine. The stone tablets on the walls and the white statue of the saint in prayer testify that this is her cell, the sacred and blessed place of her "dwelling with the eternal Spouse."[1]

Anyone who knows only, or mainly, the excellent mission of the great Sienese as ambassador, counselor, peacemaker for souls that unfolded in her full maturity, may have difficulty realizing the long path she traversed and the many obstacles she overcame to arrive at that point. She does this without betraying the principles and attractions that are at the foundations of her spirituality.

51

The first ideal of sanctity which attracts the soul of Catherine as a child of six or seven years is that of the Fathers of Egypt. Flowing from a great love for silence, there is immediately born in her the need to find a tranquil and hidden place where she can perform her exercises of piety and penance. One day, absorbed in prayer at one of her favorite places, she offers her perpetual virginity to the Lord through the hands of the Blessed Virgin Mary. She is only seven years old!

After a divine illumination and acquaintance with the Friars Preachers, her true vocation is revealed to her. She is unable to join the company of men, but through a vision or dream she decides to ask for the habit of the Order of Penance of St. Dominic [Dominican Laity]. She feels lost and broken in a large crowd of people who go about their own affairs.

The great discovery of her life, the brilliant and original intuition that she is able to actualize in every circumstance, is the Dominican synthesis of contemplation-action. She comes to this realization when she is about twelve years old. She cuts her hair to free herself from the insistence of her relatives who want to give her a husband at any cost. When Lapa becomes aware of this, it is as if lightning has struck! The entire family joins forces against the rebellious girl. In their indignation, they decide to chastise her in a way to make her become more sensible and give up her resistance.

It was decided that Catherine could no longer have a room where she could be alone… Thus she would lose a place and time to pray and unite herself to her Bridegroom.

But she was not shaken by these denials. Under the inspiration of the Holy Spirit, she fashioned within her soul a little cell which she would never leave for anything in the world. Whereas before she had a room from which she could come and go, now she made herself an interior cell that no one could take from her. She could always remain recollected there.[2]

It is difficult to determine whether the very precocious maturity of Catherine is revealed with greater clarity in the consciousness which led her to make the vow of virginity (Blessed Raymond assures us of her full knowledge despite her young age), or in the idea of constructing an indestructible cell in the heart, so cleverly intuited and tenaciously actualized.

What is certain is that her perseverance conquers every opposition. Shortly after she had created her interior cell, her family gave her back her "actual cell," that beloved secret and solitary refuge.

This little room has cold and soiled walls. Her bedding is on the hard pavement with a stone pillow. These were the images that the word "cell" first evoked in the spirit of Catherine.

Sitting and looking around the confines of the small space, the saint sees a reality of the spiritual order reflected and illuminated in every object. Her thought, transcending sensible reality, finds

> boundless
> spaces beyond that one, and
> supernatural
> silences, and the most profound
> tranquility.[3]

In those places the soul expands and is liberated from every earthly poetic fantasy to be united to God.

> Catherine "makes heaven out of her cell."[4]

Before raising her eyes above, she hastens to examine the depths of her soul. It is an almost bottomless abyss into which her gaze struggles to penetrate. It is a little like trying to follow the bucket that goes down into the well with the rope trailing behind. Finally, the bucket splashes upon the surface of the water and sinks. The pail is filled with the gurgling of the water. No matter how deep, a well ends in the earth where springs of water collect. It is the same when we begin to probe the depths of the soul which is the cell where we find God.

> It is a well which has water and earth within it. We know our misery in the earth. We realize that we are nothing. Since we are "not," we see that our being is from God. O ineffable burning charity, I see that earth and living waters are found here, that is, true knowledge of his sweet and true will that wants nothing other than our sanctification. We, therefore, enter into the depths of this well, dwelling within and knowing ourselves and the goodness of God.[5]

The knowledge of these two extremes — "I am He Who is, you are she who is not" — is wonderfully grounded in the incarnation of the Word for our salvation. It does not remain a cold, abstract concept, but is translated into love; rather, the double name of hatred-love: love for God, hatred for everything that separates from God. Therefore, the well water is a living water: the driving force of our wills. This water is the knowledge of God's will that wants us to be saints and why he gave himself for our sanctification.

> The heart immediately elevates itself by burning desire… seeing that it can reach true virtue in no other way except by

charity for one's neighbor. This charity is drawn from the knowledge of God. In the goodness of God it sees and acknowledges that God's boundless love is not only for him, but for every creature that has reason, friends and enemies.[6]

In this way the neighbor becomes the means and the stimulus for exercising the virtues for our sanctification.

You conceive love in God by seeking his honor and the salvation of souls. The love that has been conceived is tested in one's neighbor by the virtue of patience… Therefore, just as Christ endured unto death and was gloriously resurrected, so too, shall we and the other servants of God who bear with pain until the death of our sensuality. When one's sensuality is dead, grace gives the soul new life. The queen of patience gloriously destroys vice.[7]

The battle is hard and painful against the rebellion of self-love, the deceptions of the devil, the murmurings of neighbors to whom we try to do good. It involves "pain and disgrace, mockery and insult, temptations from the devil and the flesh, the tongues of murmurers and the flattery of a deceitful heart that thinks one thing and says another."[8] But it is better "to remain in the cell with

56

this war than to be outside of the cell in peace."⁹
Peace here on earth is not to seek self by fleeing
the battle, but the conscious and courageous ac-
ceptance of our situation.

Catherine writes to a nun of the monastery
of St. Abandio, or St. Bonda, as everyone in Siena
calls it. Sister Constance is tormented by scruples.
The devil is persuading her to give up the fight
and despair because nothing she does is pleasing
to God. Catherine places the truth before her eyes.

> Stir up the fire of your love, dearest
> daughter, and do not be confused, but
> tell yourself, "What comparison is there
> between my iniquity and the abundance
> of blood that was shed with such fire of
> love?" I want you to see well your non-
> being, your negligence and your igno-
> rance. However, I do not want you to
> see this in dark confusion, but by the
> light of the infinite goodness of God
> which you find within yourself.

Full of compassion and almost taking her by
the hand, Catherine introduces her to the holy
place which is illumined by the warm and prudent
lamplight. One finds rest here in the evening after
the toil of the fight.

> Do you know what you should do? Do
> as when you enter your cell at night to

go to sleep. When you go to your cell, the first thing you see is your bed. You first see not only what is necessary for the cell, but your eye and affection fly to the bed where you find rest. You should do the same by going to the cell of self-knowledge where I want you to open the eye of knowledge with affectionate love. Enter the cell and go to the bed. The sweet goodness of God is the bed. Take note that your being was given to you by grace, and not out of obligation. This bed is covered with a large blanket that is completely vermilion in the Blood of the bleeding and consumed Lamb. Rest here and never depart. You do not have a cell without a bed, nor a bed without a cell. Fatten your soul in this goodness of God… Therefore, I beg you for the love of Christ crucified, remain on this sweet and glorious bed of repose. I am certain that you will be able to do this if you will drown yourself in the Blood.[10]

Whoever remains constant in battle and many contradictions, "has progressed with true eagerness to the service of God and neighbor." This person can truly be called

an inhabitant of the cell of self-knowledge. In this cell is also the knowledge of God in self. There one grows fat and takes delight. In her cell she eats the food of souls with suffering and thus she has placed the table upon the cross. One reposes in the cell of the glory and praise of God and there is her bed.[11]

Thus, the dwelling of the cell with its double aspect, the knowledge of God in ourselves and the knowledge of ourselves in God, offers the soul two distinct missions: the duty of difficult and exhausting activity and the duty of repose. They are two spheres of light that mutually permeate one another as in the Dominican spirituality of contemplation and apostolate. The soul nourishes herself on truth and love, and "the first sweet Truth" dwells within her as in an earthly paradise.

You will find all of God within the cell of the soul. He gives such sweet refreshment and consolation that nothing happens that can disturb one. She has a capacity for the will of God because she has cast out of herself all self-love and everything that is outside God's will.

The soul soon becomes a garden full of sweet-smelling flowers of desire. The tree of the most holy cross is planted in the midst of the garden. There reposes the immaculate Lamb from whom flows the blood that bathes and inundates this glorious garden which contains the mature fruit of true and real virtue.

A dazzling spring invades the dim narrow cell. It is a vision that seems to have flowed from the brush of Fra Angelico or from the radiant mosaics of a Byzantine basilica. It is a triumphant vision.

> The one who has made of herself a garden of self-knowledge is strong against the entire world, because she is conformed and made one with the supreme strength. She truly begins in this life to enjoy a foretaste of eternal life. She rules the world.[12]

CHAPTER EIGHT

THE LAMP

In the darkness of night which invades Catherine's cell, objects take on various forms in the lamplight.

The lamp is the heart of the cell! If the lamp were extinguished, all would be lost in the darkness. It is the darkness of a tomb where everything, including the bed, table and vermilion blanket would be a hindrance, an obstacle.

"Whoever walks in darkness," Jesus says, "does not know where he is going." Darkness deceives; truth gives light. "I am the light of the world," says Jesus. "O Truth, ancient and new," writes Catherine, "the soul that possesses you is deprived of the poverty of obscurity. That person has a wealth of light."[1]

The flame of the lamp burns in a modest halo of light. The lamp, with the receding and convergent contours at its base, almost vanishes in the shadow of its own light.

Catherine thinks the lamp resembles the human heart. Like the lamp, the heart also is large at the top and narrows toward the bottom. The heart, too, needs to be ignited and burn. The soul, created out of love by the First Love, cannot live without love. It dies without love, like a room without a lamp.

The human heart is full of incoherence and contradictions; the flame of love does not remain alight without meeting opposition. Man holds his heart in his hand and it is his duty to hold it high. If he lets it tilt, the oil spills and puts out the flame.

> Every rational creature has this lamp, for the human heart is a lamp. Thus, if the hand of holy fear holds it upright it is supplied and all is well. But if it is in the hand of servile fear, it is turned upside-down, because he serves and loves himself and his own pleasure, and not for love of God. He puts out the light and spills the oil.[2]

Self-love cannot coexist with charity, just as darkness cannot coexist with light. If self-love has control of the lamp of the heart, it throws away the oil of humility and thus extinguishes the light of charity.

> It is a corrupt cloud which takes away all spiritual and temporal light. Temporal light, because it does not permit us to know our frailty and the lack of consistency and stability of the world... Spiritually, this blindness does not let us know

or discern the goodness of God. On the contrary, many times we interpret the opposite of what God has given us for our benefit... because we do not consider his mysteries, his tenderness, nor with what great love he gives us these things.[3]

This is exactly the antithesis of the interior cell, with its double illumination on the misery of creatures and the infinite goodness of the Creator! The consequence is terrible, eternal rejection. "These are those of whom our Savior said, 'I do not know you, I don't know who you are!'" writes the saint to the monks of St. Peter in Montecelli. "Therefore, I want you to be strong and prudent. Hold on to your heart and keep it straight as a lamp."[4]

The soul is similar to the wise virgins of the Gospel parable. A sweet and familiar intimacy completely pervades a letter in which she explains to her virgin niece, Nanna, daughter of Benincasa, the parable of the ten virgins.

> To be a bride of Christ it is necessary to have a lamp, oil and light. Do you know what this means, my daughter? The lamp is understood to be our heart, since the heart is shaped like a lamp. You can easily see that a lamp is large above and narrow below. So too, is the heart. This means that we should always be open

above, that is, having holy desires and images and continuous prayers, and always having in our minds the favors of God and especially the great favor of the blood with which we were ransomed.

Blessed Christ, my daughter, did not redeem us with gold or silver or pearls or other precious stones, but he purchased us with his precious blood. We can never forget such a great favor, but should always keep it before our eyes, with holy and sweet thanksgiving, seeing how immeasurably God loves us. He did not hesitate to deliver his only-begotten Son to a disgraceful death on the cross to give us the life of grace.

I say that the lamp is narrow below, and so is your heart. This means that your heart should be closed to earthly things. That is, it should neither desire nor love them inordinately, nor crave after more than he provides for us so that we never lack anything. In this way your heart will truly be a lamp.

But think, my daughter, that this would not be enough if there was no oil inside. By the oil, I mean that sweet little virtue of profound humility…

Humility is illumined and founded in the knowledge of our misery and God's goodness. This is the double foundation of the interior cell. It does not substitute the good oil for flattery and human praise.

> But it sells all allurements and worldly flatterers in order to buy this oil… [Therefore, to the foolish] it was said, "Go and buy oil"… almost as if to say, "You have not wanted to buy eternal life with your virginity and good works. You wanted to buy human praise. You go to buy praise so you cannot enter here!" Therefore, my daughter, watch out for human praise.[5]

When Catherine says that the oil is not enough if there is no light or flame, we are a little surprised to read, "This light is the light of the most holy faith," because elsewhere the flame is generally a symbol for charity. However, we should not forget that this letter is an instruction for her "virgin niece" who wants to be a bride of Christ. Thus we should remember Catherine's insistent prayer to obtain the fullness of faith. This prayer culminated when the Lord celebrated the mystical marriage with her on Shrove Tuesday. Her little cell became resplendent with his presence: "I espouse you to me in faith."[6]

Faith inflames and feeds the flame of love. Whoever knows more, loves more, and "as light grows, love grows and as love grows; virtues and good works increase until death."[7] Faith and love need to be translated into works. The saint insists upon this in her lesson to her niece.

> The saints say that faith without works is dead. Therefore, we need to continue virtuously to accomplish them. Remain no longer a worldly youth, but be a faithful bride consecrated to Christ crucified. In this way we will have the lamp and oil and light.[8]

With this light burning at the top of the heart, everything has its rightful place and spiritual meaning just as every object in the cell is lighted by the lamp. A person no longer has the temptation to follow false judgments, but enjoys everything. She is happy because she acknowledges God's will, full of love, as the cause of everything.

> O how blessed is this soul who, by the sweet knowledge of truth, has come to such light and perfection. She sees and realizes that what God permits, comes from his special love. He who is this Love, cannot help but love his creature that has reason. He loved us before we were…[9]

It does not burn of itself, but radiates its light, "illumined by God's sweet will, it gives light by the light of faith." The light acquired "in the light of true love" enables the soul to reach "true and perfect purity," because it has cast off all darkness of self-love and every disturbance, flooding it with the serene light of God. Catherine exults in the victory of light, in the victory of her Beloved.

> O glorious light! O drowned soul, lost in the light, you do not see yourself for your own sake, but you see only the light within you, and in that light you see and judge.[10]

He conquers, not in order to lose, but to save. The one who loses self in God rediscovers self in his most true and perfect reality.

Catherine lived for many years in this light of truth in which "the soul is inebriated, enjoying God by the affection of charity, with the light of the most holy faith,"[11] so she can speak with authority. Nanna is little more than a child, but she, like Catherine, is also chosen to be a true bride of Christ crucified. This explains the moving tenderness of "my daughter," so often repeated, and the firmness of the teaching.

> Thus, considering that this was the excellent way, I said that I desired to see you a true bride of Christ crucified. And so I beg you and command you to be clever. I say no more. Abide in the holy sweet love of God. Sweet Jesus, Jesus love.[12]

CHAPTER NINE

THE GARDEN

The little window in Catherine's cell opens on the side of the Camporegio hill. On the grassy hillside, perhaps in the small terrace now enclosed by the Peruzzi gallery, the Benincasas had a little vegetable garden. A garden like so many others, green even in winter with rows of plants for salad, and perfumed in the spring by the flowers of beans and peas, with an almond, peach or apple tree to stand guard, and rose bushes along the sides of the footpaths.

It is a short distance from the house to the garden. Jacob and his children go there in the evening to get some fresh air. It is refreshing after a weary day closed up in the dye shop to hoe, plant and water in the fresh, cool breeze coming from the Piatta Valley. "They [with imperfect love] are like a person in a garden who, because it gives him pleasure, finds contentment in doing the work but his contentment is really in the pleasure the garden gives him."[1]

Yes, it is wonderful to turn the earth over

69

with a spade; level it with a rake; remove the rocks and weeds; clear the rows; build up the sides with the hoe. Then, with the packages of seeds in hand, to decide to plant onions here and endive there, and cabbage over there; to scatter the seeds as one must, neither too densely nor too thinly; to build up a mound of earth and quickly water the seed so that it will put out roots and fasten itself in the earth so the ants do not carry it away. Then, when the tiny, tender lettuce-leaf sprouts are grown hiding all the dirt, to say to the women, "You can cut this; not that, I want to transplant it." It is a joy to see the leaves that at first wither, but then re-gain strength in the new soil. And finally, when the plant has given all that it can give, to uproot it and turn it under into the ground again and decide upon the next planting.

It is satisfying work. Satisfaction is in exer-cising one's own creativity in arranging things, collaborating with nature and dominating it at the same time.

And ourselves?

> We are a field where God by his mercy has thrown his seed, that is, love and affection with which he created us… He gave us the water of holy baptism so that this seed produces fruit and nour-ishes the plants.

> This fruit is sweet and exquisite. It needs a gardener who will manage it and pre-

serve its fruit. O Jesus, sweetest love,
you gave us the most vigorous and gracious gardener that we could have, reason and free will... Time has also been
given, for without time this laborer would
not be able to do anything. But with time,
that is, while we live, this laborer can till
the soil and gather the fruit. The hands
of love for holy and true desire pick the
fruit and store it in the barn, that is, in
God, performing and directing its every
activity to the praise and glory of God.[2]

The garden of the soul progresses under the
hand of this vigorous and gracious gardener, as
did that of the Benincasas because of their care.
In this way the garden is truly a place of delight,
beauty, harmony. There is a natural affinity with
the religious life which presupposes the "order of
reason."[3] Catherine frequently compares religious
life to a garden, abundant in sweetness and beauty,
as, for example, when she writes to the monks of
Cervaia.

You are invited, dearest brothers, to this
perfection, drawn out of the secular state
by the Holy Spirit, bound with the cord
of holy and true obedience, allowed to
eat the apples in the garden of holy
Church.[4]

The image of the garden spontaneously over-shadows that of the ship when Catherine contemplates the perfect order with which her father Dominic designed his ship. "He made his ship very spacious, gladsome and fragrant, a most delightful garden."[5]

Later, after the beginning of the schism, while at Rome thinking of "those glorious martyrs who went gladly to the place of martyrdom," she feels the tormented need to labor in the garden of holy Church, even to the complete sacrifice of herself. The saint wrote the following to Blessed Raymond at the end of 1378.

> We offer ourselves dead in the garden of holy Church; and for Christ on earth, the owner of this garden, we say the Office of the Dead. A dead person neither sees nor hears nor feels. Strive to kill yourself with the knife of hatred and love, so that you will not hear the mockery, insults and reproaches that the persecutor of holy Church would like to make. The eyes do not see the impossible things to do, nor the torments to come; but they see with the light of faith that through Christ crucified you can do everything… With the support of love one loses sensuality; and thus, dead, we nourish ourselves in this garden… With love for virtue, we gladly throw ourselves to the tongues and hands of brutal men.

Thus they may do with us what they did
to the others who worked and died in
this sweet garden, watering it with their
blood, after their tears and sweat. And I
— my sorrowful life! — since I did not
put forth water, refused to put out blood.
I do not want it like this anymore, let us
renew our lives and increase the fire of
desire.[6]

The ardent fire is rekindled in Catherine's
soul by that land which seems to her to boil in the
blood of the martyrs.

The blood of these glorious martyrs here
in Rome, inasmuch as their bodies are
buried, with such fire of love gave their
blood and life out of love for Life, all of
it boils, inviting… to endure for the glory
and praise of God's name and holy
Church… So, in this holy land… God
manifested his dignity by calling it his
garden.[7]

St. Catherine also calls this land "the garden
of the blessed Christ and source of our faith,"[8] in
the same sense in which Dante called Italy "the
garden of the empire." The little enclosed garden
of her childhood, the few plots of earth wedged
between the houses and the steep embankment
of the Camporegio hill, has been transformed in
the open horizon of Rome into a field. The bound-

less field of the universal Church which extends beyond one's vision and embraces the generous garden of souls "in order to turn the earth upside down, that is, to turn a disordered life into an ordered one, uproot vices and plant virtues."[9]

Jacob and his children work for enjoyment in the little garden behind the house. Catherine does so and will continue until the end of her strength. "I... have been placed in the field where blood was shed for love of the blood... I will never cease to labor."[10]

CHAPTER TEN

THE TREE

Among the plants flourishing in the Benincasa garden, there is one which especially attracts the gaze and thought of Catherine. The tree growing in the middle is the ruler of the place! Its trunk thrusts towards the heights, spreading its branches in the blue sky so that they hang over everything else. Its luxuriant leaves are secure from anything creeping on the ground. Its wood is an image of everlasting life in contrast to the ephemeral life of the green vegetables growing at it's foot.

The tree is, for Catherine, an image of God and the soul. God revealed himself to Catherine under this figure at the beginning of her spiritual formation.

> You know I showed myself to you under the image of a tree. You could see neither its bottom nor its top. But you saw that its root was joined to the earth — and this was the divine nature joined to the earth of your humanity. At the foot

of the tree, if you recall, there was a thorn bush. All who were in love with their own sensuality backed off from that thorn bush and ran away to a hill of chaff, in which I symbolized for you all the pleasures of the world. The chaff looked like grain but that is not what it was. So, as you saw, many souls died of hunger there. But many, when they recognized the world's deceit, returned to the tree and crossed through the thorn bush.[1]

Allegorical poetry, if you wish, but charged with all the pathos of a drama in which the saint profoundly lives the reality: human life destined for happiness through union with God, human life if distanced from God has no further good. "So think of the soul as a tree made for love and living only by love."[2] The tree lives by nourishment drawn from the earth. The soul finds an infinite supply of this life-giving food in true and humble knowledge of self and God.

> The circle in which this tree's root, the soul's love, must grow is true knowledge of herself, knowledge that is joined to me, who like the circle has neither beginning nor end... This knowledge of yourself, and of me within yourself, is grounded in the soil of true humility, which is as great as the expanse of the circle (which is the knowledge of yourself united with me, as I have said)...

So the tree of charity is nurtured in humility and branches out in true discernment. The marrow of the tree... is patience, a sure sign that I am in her and that she is united with me.

This tree, so delightfully planted, bears many fragrant blossoms of virtue. Its fruit is grace for the soul herself and blessing for her neighbors... To me this tree yields the fragrance of glory and praise to my name, and so it does what I created it for and comes at last to its goal, to me, everlasting life.[3]

But if the soul is "without this divine love, which is true and perfect charity, death would be her fruit instead of life."[4] The Lord grieves with Catherine,

I made them of love through the life of grace, ... they have become trees of death...

Do you know where this tree of death is rooted? In the height of pride, which is nourished by their sensual selfishness. Its core is impatience and its offshoot is the lack of any discernment...

The fruits of such trees are full of death, for their juice comes from the root of pride.[5]

Absurd like a tree with its roots in the air, is the position of people who, instead of rooting themselves in the good soil of a sincere and humble knowledge of self and God, seek the empty and unstable pleasures of the world, and "grope their way through the river as if they were blind, not seeing how completely undependable the water is."[6] Pride has shown them the flower of glory, only to creep in and corrode from within, like the grub worm that eats away at the tree — passersby do not realize it until the leaves wither.

> Alas, alas! The blind sight of our pride and greatness shows us the flower of position and power. We do not see the consuming worm that has entered beneath this plant which gave us the flower... Alas, ... the worm could grow so large that it could uproot the flower.[7]

So the tree, symbol of life, can become a symbol of death. Did not Jesus compare himself to the green wood and sinners to the dry?

There was a tree of death at the beginning of human history. After many centuries of waiting there was a tree of life that liberated humanity from death. Catherine seems to relive the anguish of the ancient patriarchs in the expectation of the new and holy shoot when she writes,

> We see the sweet desire that those holy and venerable Fathers had awaiting the coming of the Son of God. Therefore, confound and extinguish within us our ignorance and coldness and negligence.

I say "we" who have tested and seen and felt the fire of divine charity. O, what an admirable thing this is! They rejoiced only in the thought, and now we see God grafted into our flesh and made one thing with humanity, and we are not offended. O sweet and true graft! He made humanity fruitful since it was sterile, not sharing the water of grace. Therefore, whoever spreads out the wings of holy desire and fixes himself to the tree of the holy cross, will find this holy and sweet graft of the Word Incarnate of the Son of God.[8]

He "was shown to us as a tree in our humanity, full of sweet and exquisite fruits; because we were wild trees we could not be grafted into him." In fact, we "are unfruitful trees ourselves" if we are not grafted onto "the fruitful tree of the most holy and sweetest cross."[9]

The tree of the cross allegory assumes new, more profound and living significance. The soil of our humanity becomes the material from which divine Love makes the instrument of his Passion and our Redemption spring up. "We were that rock where the cross was fastened and held."[10]

If the creature matures in her soul the fruits of truth and love in humble self-knowledge before her Creator, how much more does she grow from this burning knowledge of the love that redeemed her! Therefore, pick the fruit that satisfies hunger from no other branch but the branches of the tree of the cross.

> What are these sweet fruits beneficial for us to gather? I say that it is necessary to have the fruit of true patience. This fruit should be so mature that one is never moved by impatience or ingratitude or ignorance. Like a lover, he endured and bore our iniquities on the wood of the most holy cross. There you will find this fruit that gives life to those who are dead, light to those who are blind, and health to those who are sick. This is the fruit of the most holy charity that was the bond that held God to the cross. For neither the nails nor the cross would have been sufficient to hold him fastened, but only the bond of love. Therefore, these fruits are well ripened.[11]

Salvation and a secure refuge from every snare are found in the tree of the cross.

> There, no demon, visible or invisible, can take away from us the life of grace, because being raised on high, the earth cannot impede us, as the mouth of Truth said, "If I will be lifted up, I will draw all things to myself." Thus he draws the

heart and soul and will, with all their strength.[12]

It is in the place of peaceful repose that the soul experiences how much she lost the fear of pain, the only real cause of our every disturbance. To disarm this fear, Christ crucified made of himself the way and staircase by which we can ascend. "O, to see such consummated love, who made of himself, that is, his body, a stairway to elevate us from the way of pain and put us at rest." Even if the beginning is difficult, the soul "experiences such peace and tranquillity that, [having reached the summit], like something raised on high, no bitterness can touch it. He is that peaceful bed where the soul reposes."[13]

The soul that has found the fountain of life at the tree of the cross lacks nothing.

"Therefore our hearts explode and burst gazing upon such fire and flame of love that God has grafted into man and man in God. O, love unspeakable! If the human person knew its value, it would be enough."[14]

"I say no more. Abide in the holy and sweet love of God, always resting in the branches of the true tree of that most holy cross. Sweet Jesus, Jesus Love."[15]

CHAPTER ELEVEN

THE HEDGES BETWEEN THE FIELDS

The years Catherine lived as a hermit in the solitude of her cell were a preparation for intense activity. Tempered by a rigorous silence, her words would reach people of every class and every land.

Now Catherine is frequently outside the home. Her Spouse had invited her to leave her room to serve her neighbor, walking with both feet in the way of love. Like the other Mantellate, she goes every day to care for the sick at the Camporeggio hospital or at the Scala hospital in front of the cathedral. Sometimes she cares for the poor lepers of St. Lazarus outside the Roman Gate.

The road descends from the Roman Gate between gentle rolling hills. An autumn wind swells Catherine's black mantle, turns the green olive leaves to show their silver side, and pulls on the vine branches heavy with leaves and grape clusters.

In the valley basin a plowman shouts at the oxen while he bends to thrust the plow into the sod. For hours he draws the furrows from one end of the field to the other. Catherine finds him at his slow, uniform, heavy work when she returns on the road toward the city. This kind of perseverance is necessary for the soul's progress! Catherine meditates on a Gospel verse.

> It is nothing to begin and put one's hand to the plow. Holy thoughts begin to plow and perseverance in virtue finishes it. The one who plows turns over the earth. So too, the Holy Spirit overturns the soil of the perverse sensual will. Many times a person, fascinated by the sweet invitation… seeks to find himself a good cutting plowshare to chop up his soil better. He sees and discovers that nothing is perfect at breaking and cutting and leveling the will as much as the iron yoke of holy obedience. Then, when found, he learns from the obedient Word, the Son of God, and because of his love for him wants to be obedient unto death.[1]

But how many people know how to persevere? Catherine mourns, "Alas, alas, I see that we are unfruitful earth letting the seed of the word of God be strangled by the thorns and thorn-bushes of disordered affections and desires for the world, going by way of its pleasures."[2]

During the cold months everything seems dead, immobilized by the ice, as a soul from the coldness of self-love. At the end of winter when the reddish-brown earth can again be seen under the still sparse and tender green wheat, the hedges are only an entanglement of bare thorns. Already there is a forecast of rebirth in the air. The soul also aspires to renew itself. "Let us no longer be negligent for the time of flowers has come."[3]

The March wind, impregnated with the perfume of violets and lilies, brushes the white petals of the thorn bush spreading its seed among the green wheat like an innocent seed. Gabriel's greeting vibrates in the March breeze and resounds within Catherine's heart.

> O, Mary, fruitful earth, You, Mary, are that new plant from which we have the fragrant flower of the Word, the only-begotten Son of God. In you, fruitful earth, was sown this Word. You are the earth and the plant.[4]

> Truly, in this blessed and sweet field of Mary was this Word grafted into her flesh as the seed that is thrown on the ground. It sprouts from the sun's heat and brings forth the flower and fruit, and the seed-hull remains in the earth. So too, by the heat and fire of divine charity God was truly joined to the human race, throwing the seed of his word into the field of Mary. O blessed and sweet Mary. You gave us the flower of sweet Jesus![5]

The sun's splendor and black clouds alternate in the sky by a gust of the March wind. The date of the Incarnation of the Word frequently coincides with the celebration of the mysteries of his passion.

> And when did this sweet flower produce the fruit? When he was grafted on the wood of the most holy cross we received perfect life. And why did we say that the seed-hull remains in the earth? What was this seed-hull? It was the will of the only-begotten Son of God... clothed with desire for the honor of the Father and our salvation. This immeasurable desire was so strong that he ran like a lover... to the shameful death on the cross... The same was in Mary. She could desire nothing except the honor of God and the salvation of creatures... She herself would have made a ladder to put her Son on the cross, if there had been no other way. This was all because the Son's will remained in her.[6]

We always need to remember "the teaching of Mary and that sweet First Truth." Let us study to be "vessels of election full of the fire of the most ardent charity, to carry the sweet name of Jesus and sow this sweet incarnate word of Christ in the field of souls." So that the task will not seem too difficult for us, "gently inebriate and bathe ourselves in the blood of Christ crucified, so that bitter things seem sweet, and great burdens, light; from the thorns and tribulations we draw the rose, peace and tranquility."[7]

Roses soon cover the hedges and it will seem almost incredible that under that veil of delicate petals the thorns can still be there. The soul, renewed by the paschal mysteries, will sing anew the "alleluia" of Christ's triumph in expectation of the victory that also awaits her in him and through him. Catherine will continue to travel up and down the road outside the Roman Gate working for the lepers of St. Lazarus with "hunger to reach her goal." Like a wayfarer who has no other desire than to take the most direct path, she knows that she will not have peace until she has arrived.

> Desire makes her run along the way, the beaten path of Christ crucified... It is neither dark nor gloomy nor full of thorns, but enlightened with the true light... It has no thorns for us. It is fragrant, full of thorns, flowers and exquisite fruits. It is so great that as the creature begins to keep to this road and sweet way, it tastes so much sweetness that it chooses to die rather than depart from the path. And so, if we see thorns on this path, ... I say they do not concern the soul that delights in this road. She acts as one who goes to a rose garden to

pick a rose and leave the thorn. She leaves the trials and anguish of the world behind and gathers the fragrant rose of true and holy patience. She places herself before the eye of knowledge, the blood of the Lamb, which gives life and is the guide on this road.[8]

"He would be too crazy to leave the rose for fear of the thorn!" Truly, too crazy because he would lose the rose to avoid the thorn. Wiser instead is the one who "enjoys everything and breathes the rose's fragrance."[9]

The rose is charity that blossoms in praise of God for the trials of life. Jesus, the immaculate flower of the Virgin Mother, offered perfect praise to the Father on the cross in the scarlet of his blood, in the thorns of his crown. Following his example, every soul "enduring, conquers" because tribulations "produce flowers and fruits: flowers of glory and praise of the name of God."[10]

The flowers of praise are preserved for God with jealous care; to the human person remain the fruits. If someone wanted the flowers for himself, there would no longer be "fragrant flowers giving off their perfume in the sweet presence of God," but smelly flowers like those rotten in water.[11]

"The flower... that he has picked immediately loses its beauty."[12]

CHAPTER TWELVE

THE NEEDLE AND THE DRESS

Run, run, for time is short and the road is long. And if you had everything in the world, time would not wait for you but run its course."[1]

Did Catherine perhaps have a premonition of the short span of years assigned for her life? Possibly. But what was certainly very much alive in her was the sense of the rapid flow of time — a rapidity we naively believe we have discovered as a unique aspect of our modern life.

Catherine almost has an urgency about time that flies, that escapes and alludes our activity. "We are all wayfarers and pilgrims on the road of the teaching of Christ crucified." It is necessary then to think of his Blood so that we grow "in love, in holy fear and in hunger for time."[2] "O thief, ignorant debtor," she writes to a man engulfed in sin, "Do not expect any more time. Make a sacrifice to Christ crucified of your mind, soul and body. You should give God your heart and soul and affection with all promptness, and not negligence." "This point of time" is precious because it can be enough for conversion and pardon. Considering the effort to reform virtuous attitudes after a long habit of vice, the thought of the shortness of time can be a relief. "If your frailty annoys you... say, 'My soul, endure this little pain today... perhaps your life will end tomorrow. And if you are still alive, do what you will do for God. Do this today.'" What is to be done, do quickly, this is important. "And do not delay or wait for time, because time will not wait for you."[3]

> For the love of God, we no longer wait for time! Because time is taken from our hands and man does not realize it. It is not even good sense for a person to wait for what he does not have and lose what he has.[4]

Love is the stimulus to action. Tepidity is for the one who closes his eyes to God's blessings. "For if we saw them, our hearts would burn with the fire of love and we would be starved for time."[5] The greater and more important the work is for the cause of God and souls, so much more urgent is the necessity for action. Thus, Catherine writes to Pope Gregory XI,

> ...ignite the fire of holy desire to want to act. And do not delay... your coming... I tell you, father in Christ Jesus, that you come roasted like a meek lamb. Respond to the Holy Spirit who calls you. I tell

you: come, come, come and do not wait
for time, for time does not wait for you.[6]

To Stephen Maconi she says,

I write you with desire to see you with
such light and knowledge that you will
see what you need to cut off and what
not to release. For whoever does not cut,
always remains bound, and whoever
does not flee, always remains caught...
Answer, respond, negligent son. Open
the door of your heart. What a great insult
it is for God to stand at the door of your
soul and it not be opened to him.[7]

She is impatient to burn bridges, to over-
come obstacles almost on the wings of desire.
There is nothing romantic or dissolute in this attitude. It is the logical consequence of a clear vision
matured, perhaps, in the very patient and slow
work which occupies a woman's hand. "Time is
no more than the point of a needle."[8]

What does Catherine sew as she studies the
point of the needle that enters and exits the material in such a way that it escapes from view like the
unfathomable present moment? Perhaps the "bag"
she uses to aid the poor? She keeps it sewn under
her tunic and one day it was filled with eggs to
take to "a certain poor man who suffered from
hunger because he had voluntarily distributed his

91

earthly goods for the love of God." There was also a thimble with the eggs. When Catherine entered a church to pray along the way she went into ecstasy. The weight of her completely abandoned body on her "bag of charity" broke the brass thimble and left the eggs intact.[9]

Or is she mending the clothes of her father, brothers or nephews? Or her own clothes? Mending an old dress is a little like trying to cover up one's hidden faults with excuses. Excuses that do not deceive an expert eye. "You had many patches to cover, unfaithful weaknesses, but you did not do it so I no longer see them. I think it is good if they are seen by no one but me."[10]

Or does she lend a hand to finish the splendid wedding dress for some young woman in her home who is going to a wedding? Truly, she seems to have meditated lovingly and at length on the significance of the wedding gown, like an artist who looks lovingly at her work as it slowly comes to perfection under her hands.

When she says, the "real garment of the most ardent charity... covers nudity and hides shame, and heats and consumes the cold," she thinks of that precious dress with which the Lord clothed her after she clothed him in the person of the poor man. That garment was taken from his side and sufficiently protected her from the heat and the cold.[11] What was the material effect of that mystical dress if not a sensible manifestation of what charity produces invisibly in the soul, making it indifferent, that is, divested of selfish love and clothed anew with divine love? It is necessary to divest ourselves of the old rags if we want to clothe ourselves in a precious garment. The wedding gown would be too similar to a clumsy caricature if the bride attempted to put it on over her ordinary clothes!

Babies do not have to divest themselves when they go for the first time to ask for the precious garment at the baptismal font. They are naked until the white garment clothes them in grace and the beautiful likeness with God in whose image they are created. The pure garment is enough for them to enter the wedding feast of eternal life as "they die in childhood."

> But we brides who have a space of time, if we do not put on a garment of love for the eternal Spouse, knowing his unspeakable love, we could say that this grace that we received in baptism made us naked.

We need an intelligent and strong love, tempered in adversity and the exercise of virtues, if we are to be guided by a love infused with grace. Then the soul finds herself clothed and deprived of the shame of her nudity.

I say that the shame is hidden in two ways. First, the soul casts off the shame of sin because of displeasure… I also say that another shame is taken away, that of selfish self-love and worldly appearance. The will, dead to itself and everything transitory, does not see shame. It even delights in disgrace, torments, mockery, insults, reproaches. It is happy for the honor of God that the world persecutes it with much abuse, the devil with many temptations and annoyances, the flesh with the desire to rebel against the spirit. It rejoices in everything out of revenge and self-hatred, in order to be conformed with Christ crucified… and it is not ashamed. Clothed in the garment of the supreme and eternal will of God, it is reverent and receives it with love, because it sees that God permits it out of love… It is therefore sweet to desire disgrace, for with this it traps shame.

The dress, then, is made precious like a decorated jewel, like the drops of blood that tinted the seamless robe of the Lord during his passion.

These will be the decorations that you will wear on the real garment. You know well that the eternal Spouse did the same. Over his garment he put many pains, beatings, tortures, derisions and insults and finally the disgraceful death on the cross.

Protected like this from the ice of egoism and immersed in a fire of burning charity that shows itself "by intense desire for the honor of God and the salvation of neighbor," in promptness to confront every labor, in a profound and unchanging peace, the soul is a true bride, "clothed in a wedding garment."[12]

As a true bride, she walks in the shadow of her Bridegroom, holding his teachings close to herself like a precious dress.

> This is his teaching: to bear with patience and resist with the weapons of hatred and love. O sweet and exquisite teaching! It is the treasure he chose for himself and left to his disciples. He left it as the greatest riches he could leave... Because the wisdom of the Word Incarnate saw and knew that this was the best part, he immediately loved it, and was clothed out of love. His servants and children do the same.[13]

> The treasure of charity bears interest for the treasury of time. This is the state of divine charity that always works and is never tired. It always earns time for him like a money-lender. If he sleeps, it earns. If he eats, it earns. Whatever he does, it

earns and never loses time. The money-
lender does not do this, but the treasure
of time. It is likewise for the beloved bride
of Christ burning with divine charity. She
always profits. She sleeps and charity
labors; eating, sleeping, keeping a vigil,
whatever she does, she gathers fruit from
everything. O Charity full of happiness…
you are rich above all riches.[14]

Catherine concludes,

Therefore, as true children put on this
garment. Act in such a way that it becomes incarnate and never leaves you
except when you depart from this life.
Then we will abandon the garment of
suffering and will receive the garment of
delight.[15]

Wedding dress, robe of charity, garment of
which we can repeat with the Apostle, *Induimini
Dominum nostrum Iesum Christum* (Put on our
Lord Jesus Christ), since the teaching of the Word
is the Word himself! Catherine contemplates him
as the sharp point of the needle penetrates the
material and her heart already has a foretaste of
the blessed moment when "clothed in the wedding garment we will reach the wedding feast of
eternal life with the Bridegroom."[16]

CHAPTER THIRTEEN

THE BRIDEGROOM

The dress is for the bride to adorn herself in the eyes of the bridegroom. "You know, my most beloved daughter, that the bride adorns and clothes herself when she goes before the bridegroom. She especially adorns herself and wears the color ruby-red to please her spouse. I want you to do the same."[1]

To whom does Catherine write? Perhaps to one of her nieces, a new bride? No, the letter is addressed "to a nun of the Monastery of St. Agnes in Montepulciano."

The analogies between human love and divine love, between the earthly marriage and the union of the soul with God in charity, are frequent in Sacred Scripture. Catherine's pen expresses it as a spontaneous relationship surrounding a vibrant reality.

Humanity is the bride of Christ. Fixing her eye "on the wheel of the sun, the eternal Father, she saw the Word whom he placed beside himself and gave him the human race as a bride,"[2] in the depths of his council for the redemption of humanity. The Savior's circumcision was a hint at the mystery of this mystical union. Here is its first pledge in the initial shedding of his blood anticipating the complete donation of himself on Calvary.

> Well, you see that you are a bride and that he has espoused you; you and every creature, not with a silver ring, but with a ring of his flesh. See that sweet little Word, who on the eighth day, when he was circumcised, gave up enough flesh for a ring. O abyss and unspeakable height of charity, how greatly you love this bride, the human race! O Life by which everything lives! You snatched humanity from the hands of the devil who possessed it as his own... and you espoused it with your flesh. You gave your blood as a pledge, and then later, opened your body and made the full payment.[3]

Faithful to the bride given him by the Father, he remained strong and persevering to the end. He returned the bride of the human race to the hands of the eternal Father.[4]

The Church is the bride of Christ. But what sadness to see her deprived of that deep red color that should make her pleasing to her Spouse, the deep red of charity for which he gave her his own blood as a dowry. Selfish love has made it fade in too many of her members. Those who should have shouted at the wolf have become lazy and speechless.

> Shepherds sleep because of selfish love for themselves… They are inebriated with pride. They sleep and do not see that the devil, the infernal wolf, is taking away their life of grace, and even those who are subject to them. They are not careful, and all because of the perversity of self-love. O, how dangerous this love is in prelates and subjects! If he is a prelate and selfish, he does not correct his subjects. He who loves himself for himself falls into servile fear and does not recover… Alas, be silent no longer. Cry out with a hundred thousand tongues. I see that because of silence the world is ruined, the bride of Christ has turned pale. Her color is gone because the blood has been sucked from behind her back… Alas, I die and I cannot die.[5]

In her love for the divine Bridegroom, Catherine suffers profoundly the evils in the Church. "For what would it mean to me to have eternal life if death were the lot of your people, or if my faults especially and those of your other creatures should bring darkness upon your bride, who is light itself?" To her ardent prayer for mercy for

the Church, God promises to restore the beauty
of the Bride of Christ by much suffering.

> Bring, then, your tears and your sweat,
> you and my other servants. Draw them
> from the fountain of my divine love and
> use them to wash the face of my bride. I
> promise you that thus her beauty will be
> restored. Not by the sword or by war or
> by violence will she regain her beauty,
> but through peace and through the con-
> stant and humble prayers, and sweat and
> tears poured out by my servants with
> eager desire.[6]

"The disciple is not greater than his master."[7] The Bride of Christ will not recapture her
beauty except with the money that has already
poured out from him to purchase her for himself.

In one sense, the bride of Christ is especially
the soul consecrated to him. The Bridegroom gave
Catherine a special privilege by irrevocably unit-
ing her to himself, with full knowledge at the age
of seven. She loves with a love jealous for souls
consecrated to him. The analogy of an earthly
marriage is useful to herself and to them. She acts
like someone who knows what she is talking about
because she lives what the analogy represents.
Thus, she affirms that "the state of the bride is to
become one will with her bridegroom, and to want
nothing but what he wants and to think of nothing

but him."[8] Catherine expresses that happy identi-
fication of thought and affection that makes one
heart of two. At the same time she anticipates
what the liturgy will say of her, "no one could love
Christ more."[9]

Her love is jealous because of Christ's jealous love for these souls chosen and put in a privileged position by him. There is great delicacy in
maintaining strict vigilance to avoid a fall that would
change honor into dishonor. Catherine writes to
her niece, Sister Eugenia.

> Consider that your Spouse, Christ sweet
> Jesus, does not want anything between
> you and him. He is very jealous. As soon
> as he sees that you love something be-
> sides himself, he will leave you. Then
> you would deserve to eat the food of
> animals [instead of] enjoying the angelic
> food [of divine love]...
>
> So that this will never happen, be care-
> ful that you do not have the misfortune
> of having special conversations, whether
> religious or secular. If I should know or
> hear of such things, and even if I am not
> present, I will give you such a discipline
> that you will remember it the rest of your
> life... Be strong and mature... When
> guests come and ask for you at the grille,
> remain in peace and do not go if the
> prioress does not command you under

obedience. So bow your head and be like a wild hedgehog.[10]

Catherine surely had to laugh at the picture of a Sister at the grille with her head lowered like a hedgehog among the thorns. More than the image of the little prickly animal that she might have seen along some country road, she associates it with another comical memory of the determined attitude of some young bride in her family in the face of an annoying suitor.

Invitations to fidelity and perfect union of thought and will frequently flow from her pen. "The bride should never be out of tune with her bridegroom's will."[11] "The true bride loves nothing except her bridegroom."[12] "What greater pleasure can the bride have than to be conformed to her spouse and be clothed in a similar garment?"[13] Why turn to others when "he is that eternal bridegroom that never dies, and what can the soul desire that is not found in him? He is that sweet place where the bride fills the lamp of her heart."[14] She fills it with a fullness that includes every degree of human love in its most delightful aspects. Catherine can testify to this since she experiences it.

> The divine Bridegroom, wishing to care for me as a father for his daughter and the bridegroom for his bride, cannot bear any bitterness, but finds new ways to give happiness; so too, does the Word.[15]

The fullness of joy is in perfect fidelity and the reward is transformation in Christ.

> O, how beautiful is her soul! She has become one with her Spouse and can neither want nor desire anything but what God wants. While she thus sweetly crosses the tempestuous sea and gives off the fragrance of virtue in the garden of holy religion, someone might ask Christ crucified, "Who is this soul?" He would say, "She is another me, made so by the affection of love." She has the wedding garment and is not cast out of the wedding feast, but is received by the eternal Bridegroom with joy and gaiety. She gives off a perfume, not so much before God, as before the evil people of this world, so that they owe her reverence whether they want to or not.[16]

The invitation to the "wedding feast of eternal life" is not only for some privileged souls. "Blessed Christ has invited us all, and he has given everyone the garment of his grace which we received in holy baptism."[17] Therefore, the bride of Christ is every soul whom he leads to perfect union by diverse paths. Until the soul is established in this state, he acts like a lover who wants to conquer the affections of a beloved woman. Now he shows himself, now he remains at a distance, knowing that absence still more than presence will be helpful in making her realize how indispensable he has become to her.

> I told you that I come and go — leaving
> in terms of feelings, not in terms of grace
> — and I do this to bring them to perfection. When they reach perfection I relieve them of this lover's game of going
> and returning. I call it a "lover's game"
> because I go away for love and I return
> for love.[18]

A lover's game to him who holds the universe in his hand and knows the secret paths of every heart, even if to us who watch from below "unable to see beyond our noses" it can appear a drama or tragedy. A move in the divine game of love was doubtless the sentence that seemed to cast Niccolò di Tuldo into desperate rebellion. Another move was Catherine's visit which brought the condemned man back to love. It was a fullness of love that he had never known before, leaving him only the fear of not being strong at the final moment; but the boundless and burning goodness of God did not deceive him. Continuing the game of love, "he had so much affection and love in desire for me and for God, that he did not know how to remain without him."[19]

To this soul, now a *sponsa Christi*, Catherine can speak of death as a wedding feast. On the eve of Niccolò's execution she tells him, "Be consoled, my sweet brother, for soon we will arrive at the wedding feast. You will go to it bathed in the blood of the sweet Son of God, with the name of Jesus." At the moment he put his head on the block, she made the sign of the cross and repeated to him, "Down, to the wedding feast, my sweet brother, for soon you will be in everlasting life!"

It is no wonder then that precisely in this tragic circumstance Catherine gives us the most exquisite bridal image that her pen could trace. It is not a static image, but one caught in a gesture of delicate dignity and grace. It seems to pulsate with the same sentiments which the bride experiences on the threshold of her bridegroom's house at the moment she first glimpses her new world — a world desired, but still full of mystery.

Kneeling on the scaffold of "justice," Catherine takes Niccolò's bleeding head and presses it against her white habit while her spiritual gaze follows the executed man's soul in its ascent "toward its goal." She sees his violent and cruel death become precious in the blood of Christ. She sees the Incarnate Word "in the fire of his divine charity," behold the "fire of holy desire" inflamed by grace in Niccolò. Catherine sees the infinite goodness of God waiting for the soul with the indescribable sweetness of love.

The soul, now able to taste the divine sweetness after such pain, "made a sweet gesture to attract a thousand hearts. He turned like a bride, when she has reached her bridegroom's door, turns and bows her head to those who accompany her as a sign of thanks."

Catherine delights in that act of gratitude with which Niccolò's soul turns to greet her who had accompanied him to the wedding feast of eternal life as an elder sister accompanies a younger one to the home of her bridegroom. "My soul rested in peace and tranquillity." But immediately she breaks out in a cry of pain at the thought of being left on the Bridegroom's doorstep. "Alas, miserable wretch. I do not want to say any more. I remain on earth with the greatest envy."[20]

Indeed, the wedding of the soul with Christ is not only a beautiful image for her, but the most vibrant reality of her entire life.

CHAPTER FOURTEEN

THE PEACEFUL SEA

Catherine is barely 27 years old when the superior of St. Dominic's Order of Preachers calls her out of her cell, her home, her Siena, to give an account of her life to the Order's General Chapter gathered in Florence at the Church of Santa Maria Novella on Pentecost, 1374.

Thus begin those journeys which would occupy such a large part of the last six years of her life, covering many miles between Avignon and Rome.

Returning from Florence with the Order's full approval, Catherine leaves Siena again in the same year and goes to Montepulciano seeking encouragement for her mission from Agnes, the first woman Dominican saint. Immediately afterwards, in the Spring of 1375, while Catherine is in Pisa initiating her extraordinary political activity, she receives the "final impression" of the stigmata from Christ crucified.

From the Pisan court, Catherine's gaze rests for the first time upon the boundless expanse of sea. Here she leaves behind the dusty and muddy roads that rise and fall on the Tuscan hills tread by weary pilgrims. For the first time, Catherine puts her feet into a boat and entrusts herself to the Tyrrhenian Sea to cross to the Island of Gorgona.

The ship's movement, gently pulling away from the shore and sliding tranquilly on the expanse of water, gives her a sense of repose so very much appreciated after the toil of the journey. It is enough just to let oneself be carried along, gently rocked by the breeze on the waves.

Catherine's thoughts go to the monks of the Carthusian Monastery of Gorgona who have requested her visit. Their life, the life of those who enter a religious order and entrust themselves to the guidance of obedience, is similar to a ship voyage.

> I see that Divine Providence has placed you in a boat... that is, holy and true religion. That boat is guided by the yoke of holy and true obedience. Think how great is the grace that God has given you, knowing the weakness of your arms. Those in secular life navigate this sea by their own arms, but those who are in holy religion navigate with the arms of others.[1]

While she is carried gently along, Catherine contemplates the sea stretching beyond her sight to the horizon. How can one not think of the immensity of God? Leaning over the side of the boat, she tries to probe the water's depths and sees it swarming with life: fish darting about, seaweed tossed on the pattern of light refracted by the rippling waves. How could one not think of him who, unchangeable in himself, is the primary source of life for every creature? ... and of the inscrutable abyss of his eternal counsel? ... and of the Providence that gently guides every being to its goal, like the mass of water which supports and carries the ship?

Perhaps an echo of the sensations produced in her by the new spectacle is found in a letter written precisely at this time to Friar Bartolomeo Dominici.

> I invite you to enter the peaceful and profound sea through this most ardent charity. I have now discovered this anew — not that the sea is new, but it is new to me in the sentiment of my soul — in that word "God is love."[2]

If the loving soul "seems to cry out to God,"[3] how can the sea's majesty not lend new voice to the love that sings within Catherine's heart?

"O abyss! O eternal Godhead! O deep sea!" To live in this abyss, to be penetrated with this fountain of life!

You, eternal Trinity, are a deep sea: The
more I enter you, the more I discover,
and the more I discover, the more I seek
you. You are insatiable, you in whose
depth the soul is sated yet remains always hungry for you, thirsty for you, eternal Trinity, longing to see you with light
in your light.[4]

We enter tranquillity and peace at the end of
our pilgrimage in the vision revealed by God's
light.

We are pilgrims... [the Word Incarnate]
has accompanied us on our pilgrimage
and given himself to us as food to make
us run bravely, ... reaching the goal of
death we rest in bed, in the peaceful sea
of the divine essence, where we receive
the eternal vision of God.[5]

The blessed soul will then be like a

...vessel dipped into the sea [that] cannot contain the whole sea, but only as
much as it can hold. Only the sea itself
can fully contain itself. In the same way,
I [Jesus], the sea of peace, am the only
one who can fully contain and value
myself. And this makes me rejoice in
myself, and the joy and good that I have
in myself I share with you, with each of

you according to your own capacity. I fill
you and do not leave you empty.[6]

But the pilgrim soul cannot wait until that
moment without satisfying its desire. In anticipa-
tion of the vision, God introduces her into the
abyss of his mysteries by the light of faith. This
light, which is a gift of God, in some way shares in
the infinity and depth of his own light.

> You are that light beyond all light who
> gives the mind's eye supernatural light…
> and in that light receives you who are
> Light…

> Truly this light is a sea, for it nourishes
> the soul in you, peaceful sea, eternal
> Trinity. Its water is not sluggish; so the
> soul is not afraid because she knows the
> truth. It distills, revealing hidden things…
> This water is a mirror in which you, eter-
> nal Trinity, grant me knowledge; for
> when I look into this mirror, holding it in
> the hand of love, it shows me myself, as
> your creation, in you, and you in me
> through the union of the Godhead with
> our humanity which you have brought
> about.[7]

In this way, "considering oneself in the source
of the sea of the divine Essence," a person knows
what is important to know: the dignity that God

has given and whether one faithfully preserves or disfigures the imprint of the divine image.

> As he looks in the fountain he sees his image. Seeing it, he loves it and delights in it. And if he is wise he will be moved to love the fountain rather than himself. For if he had not seen it, he would not have loved it, not taken pleasure in it, nor corrected the defects of his face that he saw in the fountain... In no other way can we see our dignity, nor our defects which remove the beauty of our soul, if we do not go to look into the peaceful sea of the divine Essence.[8]

Yes, if a person is not stupid he will love God more than himself, the fountain more than the image, the sea more than one of the many things that flicker and vanish in the boat's wake. The light of faith reveals above all the supreme and infinite Good in the "sea of the divine Essence." Catherine's soul turns and exults in God.

> Good above every good, joyous Good, Good beyond measure and understanding! Beauty above all beauty; Wisdom above all wisdom — indeed you are Wisdom itself! You who are the angel's food are given to humans with burning love. You, garment who cover all nakedness, pasture the starving within your

sweetness, for you are sweet without trace of bitterness.[9]

Small, white crests scurry across the blue surface by the breath of the wind. If some break against the side of the ship, the sailors breathe deeper the salty sea air in the foam that envelops them for a moment. In a similar way, we can taste God in this life which is "less than a whiff of a droplet, a nothing in comparison to the sea."[10]

As long as we are on earth we remain wayfarers and pilgrims whether we measure our path step by step in the mud and dirt, or whether we navigate with the wind upon a restless substance. As the beautiful vision is in a certain sense anticipated by the light of faith, so too, the soul has a foretaste of resting on the "peaceful sea of the divine Essence" in the sweetness of eucharistic union.

> In communion the soul seems more sweetly bound to God and better knows his truth. For them the soul is in God and God in the soul, just as the fish is in the sea and the sea in the fish.[11]

The love in Catherine's soul is clothed anew while the ship glides across the waves toward port.

CHAPTER FIFTEEN

THE TEMPESTUOUS SEA

The calm sea, the peaceful sea, rippled by a light breeze and dotted with countless rays of light, is one of the most obvious images of the divine Essence and its life of unalterable serenity.

But when the sea swells under the fury of the wind, and the waves beat upon the shore, covering and uncovering the reefs of the deep; when they hurl themselves roaring against the rocks and crash against the high crests; when the sailors on their ships feel they are on a dry piece of straw; then the sea resembles human life more closely, even if — or precisely because — in its depths it remains undisturbed. Our life is just like this. Winds and reefs and fatigue, all of this breathtaking anxiety, and yet in the midst of all this to keep on course in the tranquil arms of the Providence of God which never ceases for an instant to sustain all that lives and to guide our tormenting events.

Salvation is allowing ourselves to be carried by these arms which never fail in power, wisdom or love. To allow ourselves to be carried means to obey. "Every reasoning creature should be obedient to God's commandments."[1]

Catherine, writing during an ecstasy to two Olivetan monks, affirms the general necessity that anyone who wants to be saved must obediently follow the way marked out by Christ. But when she passes from general obedience to particular obedience, "which those have who... follow the counsels," the saint directs her ship in the midst of the raging sea and with true obedience "navigates bravely in the tempestuous sea."

Just as on the expanse of the open sea one encounters winds that blow from different directions and converge at a point, raising up whirlpools and breaking the ship's masts, so too, in the soul the passions collide and rise up: pride, impatience, infidelity, injustice, etc. But if the wind of obedience blows constantly and is strong enough to conquer the others, the boat sails swiftly. "This little boat goes straight toward the port of eternal life with the wind of obedience and never hits a reef."

Yes, the reefs!

> Many reefs are found in the sea of this stormy life. We will crash into them if the vigorous wind of obedience is not with us. How hard is the reef of the conflicts of the devil who never sleeps [and even less, ceases sowing the seeds of

temptations along our path the more we strive to get closer to God.] … And you will also find the reef of fragile and miserable flesh that wants to do battle against the spirit… There is also the reef of the world… [This one peeks out of the waves like an enchanted island], all in bloom, even if it is constantly bitter… Its every delight and pleasure lessens as the beauty of a flower when it is picked. In the field it seems to be beautiful and fragrant but once cut, the beauty immediately fades and its perfume disappears.

Obedience evades all of this like a steersman who holds the ship on a good course with a firm hand. Fearless, "he rejoices not because he navigates by his own arm, but by the arm of the Order."[2]

The "arms of the Order" for a religious are different than "his arms." No religious can remain in the ship of religious life as a passenger; all are members of the crew. The weariness of one's arms is coordinated with the common fatigue in the rhythm appointed by mutual charity.

There is plenty of toil, but its pain is missing because the one who has lost self has also lost feeling. "As much as every labor wearies us, so much so does it seem troublesome to the will, but to the obedient who has no will, labor is a delight."[3]

Obedience establishes the soul in peace and

tranquillity of mind since "the will which causes the trouble has been taken away."[4]

> What tongue could sufficiently describe the peace of a faithful soul? I do not say she is in peace because she is deprived of every tempestuous wave on the sea; but her will is in peace because she has become one with the sweet will of God. Thus, the tempest is calm because the soul does not think of herself.[5]

This peace in the midst of a tempest is achieved by strong and firm persons, faithful in loving and acting. The weak and unreliable ones who deceive themselves about being able to navigate in the tempest by twiddling their thumbs are like the hired servant who

> raises the sail at every wind. So if it is a breeze of consolations, he moves with a light heart; and if a wind of tribulations, he moves impatiently; and if it is a wind of battle and attacks of the devil, he grows lukewarm and sits down in the weariness of a sad heart imagining that he is deprived of God when he sees his mind is void of consolations and feelings.[6]

> This is no voyage for a little bark —
> This ocean which my venturous prow
>   now cleaves —
> Nor for a pilot who would spare himself.[7]

Catherine writes to Friar Thomas della Fonte, "I write you on behalf of Christ crucified to furnish the little boat of your soul with faith and hunger." To others she writes, "The channel is open and flowing. When we need to supply the little boat of our souls, we can go furnish them there at the sweetest canal, that is, the heart and soul and body of Jesus Christ."[8]

She continues to explain herself by inviting Friar Raymond of Capua to "enter the boat of the most holy cross and fearlessly navigate the raging sea." Catherine attributes to the ideal boat a quality which is not always easy to find in ships made of wood.

> Whoever is in this little boat has no need to fear servile fear because the ship is supplied with whatever food the soul wants. If we come to contrary winds that might hit us and slow us down so that we might not be able to accomplish fully our desires, we remain with a living faith that we have food to eat. The boat is so strong that no terrible wind beating against the reef can ever break it. It is true that many times the boat is covered with the waves of the sea and fails, not because we are sinking, but because we do better and more perfectly in the peaceful time than the tempestuous one. In a time of peace we trust too much in ourselves, [acting like a hired servant who

raises the sail at every breeze]. We should
return to holy fear with humble and continual prayer, with holy and burning desire, seeking his honor and the salvation
of souls in the little ship of the cross.[9]

The boat of the Cross traverses the sea for
everyone. All are invited to embark, as everyone
is bound by obedience to the law of God. The soul
that is more concerned gives more honor to God.

Her search leads her by the light of faith
to the religious life. The Holy Spirit made
this [way of life] and set it there like a
ship ready to receive souls who want to
race on to perfection and bring them to
the port of salvation.

"The captain of this ship is the Holy Spirit"
and this is enough to explain why the boat does
not crash on the reefs. "This ship is so delightful
within that your tongue could never describe her,"
the Lord says to Catherine as he shows her the
great unity of his fleet.

Consider the great order with which
Benedict governed his ship.

Consider Francis. With what fragrantly
perfect poverty and what pearls of virtue he governed his order's ship! He
steered it along the way of high perfection...

And look at the ship of your father Dominic, my beloved son. He governed it with a perfect rule, asking [his followers] to be attentive only to my honor and the salvation of souls with the light of learning. He wished to build his foundation on this light, while not for all that giving up true and voluntary poverty...

So Dominic set his ship in order by rigging it with three strong ropes: obedience, continence, and true poverty.[10]

The captain of every ship is the Holy Spirit. Whoever gets on board entrusts himself completely to the Spirit in order to taste sweetness and security in the midst of the tempest.

If the soul on this boat is not only on the shore but throws herself into the depths of the ship, in the abyss of the crucified and ardent love of Christ crucified, [the storm] will do her no harm. Rather, she will rise up greatly comforted and strengthened wanting to endure blamelessly the pains and labors and reproaches of the world, having tasted and experienced therein Divine Providence.[11]

On the ship of obedience and the Cross, the Word was obedient unto death and ventured forth as the first to signal the course for us. Catherine, with the persuasion of her ardent love, makes this request.

> Therefore, divested of selfish love and clothed with the doctrine of Christ crucified, I beg you and want you to enter this ship of the most holy cross and sail across this tempestuous sea.[12]

The mind's eye, absorbed in contemplation of the ideal ship, has a new image of the beloved and a venerated sign of the passion and triumph of Christ on the tree of the ship. The banner is cut like a cross on the sail.

> Hold the tree of the most holy cross upright. Set sail with his most ardent charity; by this sail you will arrive at the port of salvation.[13]

The keel is almost out of sight under the tree towering like a giant. "The Cross has become the ship and the portal that guides us to the shore of salvation."[14]

Chapter Sixteen

THE HOOK AND THE NET

Catherine stands on the wharf at the port watching a point where a fishing line is submerged in the very calm surface of the water near her. The thin line jerks and bends at a tug. A sharp and quick jerk draws something out of the water, hurling it into the air: a desperate, wriggling, lightning-flash of silver scales in the sun. Off the hook, the fish still gasps in the basket. The hook, already hidden in a new piece of bait, plunges again into the water. A clear form can already be seen in the greenish liquid, gliding calmly toward the small, seemingly harmless worm that hides the snare.

Does not the same thing happen in the world of souls? For as many as fall into the traps of the devil, there are many more who are not ready to fall. Just like the fisherman seated on the shore as still as a plaster statue, he knows how to play a cunning game. He too begins by staying still and silent so as to be forgotten. When the soul feels peaceful and secure, that is the best time to assail

123

her. He does not disclose his true face, you understand. The father of lies feels stronger in the ways
of cunning and deceit. "Frequently the devil makes
us see many truths to lead us into lies."[1]

> The devil invites people to the water of
> death, for that is what he is himself. He
> blinds them with the pleasures and hon-
> ors of the world. He catches them with
> the hook of pleasure under the guise of
> good. There is indeed no other way he
> could catch them, for they would not let
> themselves be caught unless they found
> some good or pleasure in it for them-
> selves, because the soul by its very na-
> ture always craves what is good.[2]

The fish does not suspect the trap that is in
the bait. A person gifted with intellect ought to
see inside better so as not to fall because of self-
love.

> The devil, evil as he is, sees that the soul
> is blinded by sensual selfish love and pro-
> poses all sorts of sins to her. But they
> are all disguised as something profitable
> or good. And he makes different pro-
> posals to people according to their situ-
> ations and the vices to which he sees
> them most open. He proposes one thing
> to the layperson, another to the religious,
> another to priests, another to those in

authority — to all according to their different situations.[3]

Could there be anything better than charity? Certainly not. Charity, with God for its object, is so opposed to the devil (hatred itself) that it seems to be absolutely beyond the reach of his blows. But if charity is not enlightened, the devil begins to fish in the muddy waters of a confused mind.

> [The soul bites the hook] as so many imperfect souls do who let themselves be caught by the bait of love. Beginning to measure with the charity of God, that is, the love of creatures for his sake, they then leave this straight measure and fall into the measure of their own sensuality.[4]

Then devotion which should be charity's pure submission can become death's bait. "Then you would see the blind man who had lost God through the bait of devotion."[5]

It seems an absurd paradox, but it is so painfully true as to inflame within Catherine an indignation that bursts out in a curse. "O cursed devotion for exceeding your limits! O subtle bait, you enter quietly like a thief that rages..."[6]

Another fruit of charity is desire for the good of one's neighbor. It is born in the soul from the remembrance of the love for our salvation which led Christ to his death on the cross. Here also one needs clear ideas on the relationship existing between God and ourselves, between ourselves and other creatures. If humility does not shed light, zeal can be so imprudent as to send all souls along the same path, and what is worse, to measure everyone with the same yardstick, judging defective those who do not conform to the mold.

It is something truly grotesque to impose oneself as a law and standard, closing one's eyes to the beauty of the infinite variety God pleases to bring forth in the spiritual world.

This is also "the devil's deceit and malice" that one needs to guard against. "For the devil," admonishes the Lord, "would like to catch you with this inviting hook, often making you pass judgment on something that is not present in your neighbors, and so you would scandalize them."[7]

Thus, the treacherous fisherman might be able to boast of having pulled in a big fish! The soul might see herself caught in his hand by her own fault and the evil aroused in other souls by the scandal of her imprudent zeal. Perhaps others, influenced by hatred rather than love, might go to him almost without need of any other bait.

Afraid of saddening his companion, Adam became blind to the dignity in which he was created and fell into disobedience. Thus from the beginning of the world "this disobedience has been and is the source of all the evils that have come after it," since humanity was in the "hands of the devil who possessed it as his own."[8]

When the divine Goodness provided a rescue for humanity by wedding it to himself in the Incarnation, then the shrewd sower of snares, the deceitful distorter of good and evil, like a foolish little fish, bit the largest hook thrown out in the entire course of the centuries.

> I gave humankind the Word, my only-begotten Son, thus providing for your need with great prudence and providence. I say "with prudence" because with the bait of your humanity and the hook of my divinity I caught the devil, who could not recognize my Truth. This Truth, the Incarnate Word, came to destroy and put an end to his lies, which he had used to deceive humankind.[9]

> O abyss and inestimable depth of charity how much you love this spouse, the human race!... You tied the devil's hands... taking him with the hook of humanity.[10]

Humanity is free, enlightened and strong because of the victory of eternal Truth over the father of lies. The soul is so strong now as to be able to remain victorious herself in the footsteps of her Lord. If the cunning demon lays different snares according to the different inclinations, all its attempts are in vain when the light of prudence guides the soul. No matter what state the person is in, she gathers and tastes the fruits of charity. "Exquisite and of the greatest sweetness, they nourish the soul in the life of grace." Someone illumined by that glorious light "hungers for the honor of God and the salvation of souls, throwing him the hook of doctrine and an exemplary life."[11]

> Truly these last [says the Father] can be called another Christ crucified, my only-begotten Son, because they have taken his task upon themselves. He came as a mediator to put an end to the war and reconcile humanity to me in peace by suffering even to the shameful death of crucifixion. In the same way must these be crucified and become themselves mediators in prayer, in word, in good holy living, setting themselves up as an example to others. The precious stones of virtue shine in their patience as they bear others' sins. These are the hooks with which they catch souls.[12]

In first place among the followers of Christ in this holy catch of souls is his Mother.

> I have not forgotten the reverence and love he had for Mary, my only-begotten Son's most gentle mother. For my goodness, in deference to the Word, has de-

> creed that anyone at all, just or sinner,
> who holds her in due reverence will never
> be snatched or devoured by the infernal
> demon. She is like a bait set out by my
> goodness to catch my creatures.[13]

Mary, more than any other creature, knows
how to attract souls to God because, more intimately united to him and richer in grace, she is
moved by a supremely pure and right intention.

In the uprightness of a zeal that works out of
love for God and souls and with the charm of true
virtue, the catch of fish can assume proportions
so vast as to demand a more efficient means than
a simple fishing line.

Is it the reflection of the sails of the fishing
boat on the surface of the deep sea, or the remembrance of the Gospel that suggests the image?

> They throw out their nets to the right,
> not to the left... for the left hand of
> selfishness is dead in them, and the right
> is alive with a true, sincere, gentle, and
> divine love, with which they cast the nets
> of holy desire into me, the peaceful sea.

Love must be united to humility so that the
catch will be fruitful.

> They have to call out lovingly to their
> neighbors and ask them to help take in
> these soul-fishes... When they pull in the

net they take them in in great numbers. [Desire is not exhausted] because the soul who is hungry for my honor is never content with a fraction but wants them all. She asks the good to help her get the fishes into her net so that they may be preserved and become more perfect. She would have the imperfect become perfect. She would have the bad become good. The darksome unbelievers she would have turn to the light of holy baptism. She wants them all, whatever their condition, because she sees them all in me, created by my goodness in such burning love and redeemed by the blood of my only-begotten Son, Christ crucified.

So she has taken them all into the net of her holy desire.[14]

Catherine's vision extends beyond the visible horizon "for the great sea of being," in a boundless desire of life in God that embraces the universality of souls. The divine voice continues to admonish her.

I told you that Peter, at the Word's command, cast out the net. Thus he was obedient, believing with a lively faith that he could take a catch. So he caught plenty, but not during the night. Do you know what nighttime is? It is the

130

darksome night of deadly sin, when the soul is bereft of the light of grace. During this night the soul catches nothing at all, because she casts her desire not in the living sea but in the dead, where she finds only sin, which is nothingness. In vain does she wear herself out in great unbearable pain without any profit… But when the day breaks and she leaves sin behind to return to grace, the commandments of the Law appear before her mind, telling her to cast this net of hers into the word of my Word by loving me above all things and her neighbor as herself. Then in obedience and by the light of faith with firm hope she casts her net into his word by following the teaching and the footsteps of this gentle loving Word.[15]

In the perfection of charity for God and neighbor, the soul finds herself in tempered harmony since her power of attraction is divested of every material appearance and is pure music.

The soul's movements, then, make a jubilant sound, its chords tempered and harmonized with prudence and light, all of them melting into one sound, the glorification and praise of my name…

Whether the world is willing or not, the wicked cannot but feel the pleasantness of this sound. And many, many continue to be caught on this instrumental hook: They leave death behind and come to life.

All the saints have gone fishing with this organ. The first to sound forth the sound of life was the gentle loving Word when he took on your humanity. On the cross he made a sweet sound with this humanity united with the Godhead, and he caught the children of the human race. He also caught the devil, for he took away from him the lordship he had had for so long because of his sin.

All of you sound forth when you learn from this maestro. The apostles learned from him and sowed his word throughout the world. The martyrs and confessors, the doctors and virgins all caught souls with their sound. Consider the glorious virgin Ursula: She played her instrument so sweetly that she caught eleven thousand from the virgins alone, and from all sorts of folk she caught more with the same sound.[16]

The chorus of the blessed in heaven pass by in the evening's pink sunset that harmonizes heaven, earth and sea. The sails are lowered, the trawlers come to port with the nets collected in the hull near the baskets full of fish. Catherine sighs with desire: only the perfect "catch plenty and with great perfection."[17]

NOTES

Chapter 1

1. Catherine of Siena, *Le Lettere*, collected and with notes by Niccolò Tommaseo, edited by Piero Misciatelli in six volumes (Florence: C/E Giunti-G. Barbera, 1940), Letter 98. In the following notes the Letter will be indicated by "L."
2. L 217.
3. L 164.
4. L 8.
5. *Ibid.*
6. *Ibid.*
7. L 52.
8. L 59.
9. L 55.
10. L 12.

Chapter 2

1. L 204.
2. L 219.
3. L 109.
4. *Ibid.*
5. Catherine of Siena, *The Dialogue*, tr. by Suzanne Noffke, OP (New York: Paulist Press, 1980), Chapter 78, p. 147. In the following notes, chapters in the *Dialogue* will be indicated as "D - chapter number."
6. L 109.
7. L 2.
8. *Ibid.*
9. L 246.
10. L 70.
11. *Ibid.*
12. L 189.
13. *Ibid.*

Chapter 3

1. D 155, p. 330.
2. *Ibid.*, pp. 330 & 331.
3. L 69.
4. L 21.
5. L 16.
6. L 182; 225.
7. L 38.
8. D 90, p. 167.
9. Raymond of Capua, *Vita di S. Caterina da Siena
   [Legenda major]*, tr. by Giuseppe Tinagli, OP, ed. by
   Giacinto D'Urso, OP, (Siena: Edizioni Cantagalli, 1978),
   #109. In the following notes it will be indicated as *Life*.
   There is a good English translation, *The Life of
   St. Catherine of Siena*, tr. by Conleth Kearns, OP
   (Wilmington, DE: Michael Glazier, Inc., 1980) with the
   same paragraph numbers as the Italian edition.

Chapter 4

1. Tr: The Italian word for "bee" is *l'ape*. Raymond makes
   use of the pun with Lapa's name in his biography of
   Catherine.
2. Raymond, *Life*, #83.
3. *Ibid.*, #121.
4. L 92.
5. John 4:34.
6. L 259.
7. L 134.
8. *Ibid.*
9. L 52.
10. D 48, p. 98.
11. L 134; see also, "angelic food" in L 26.
12. D 41, p. 83.
13. L 69.
14. L 256.

Chapter 5

1. L 333.
2. *Ibid.*
3. L 150.
4. D 96, pp. 179-180.

5. L 260.
6. *Ibid.*

Chapter 6

1. D 131, p. 263.
2. D 129, p. 257.
3. D 142, p. 293.
4. *Ibid.*, p. 294.
5. L 283.
6. L 208.
7. D 110, p. 207.
8. *Ibid.*, pp. 207-209.
9. L 213.
10. L 226.
11. L 225.
12. Dante, *The Divine Comedy: Purgatory*, X, 45, tr. by Lawrence Grant White (New York: Pantheon Books, 1948), p. 81.
13. D 112, p. 211.
14. D 16-17, p. 55.
15. D 111, p. 210.

Chapter 7

1. L 86.
2. Raymond, *Life*, #48-49.
3. Leopardi, *L'infinito.*
4. L 203 and 215.
5. L 41.
6. L 104.
7. *Ibid.*
8. *Ibid.*
9. L 154.
10. L 73.
11. L 104.
12. L 241.

Chapter 8

1. John 12:35; 9:5; L 227.
2. L 79.
3. L 56.

4. L 79.
5. L 23.
6. Raymond, *Life*, #115.
7. L 176.
8. L 23.
9. L 173.
10. L 250.
11. L 227.
12. L 23.

Chapter 9

1. D 67, p. 128.
2. L 138.
3. L 3.
4. L 189.
5. D 158, p. 339.
6. L 344.
7. L 329.
8. L 347.
9. L 12.
10. L 344.

Chapter 10

1. D 44, pp. 90-91.
2. D 10, p. 41.
3. *Ibid.*, pp. 41-42.
4. *Ibid.*, p. 41.
5. D 31, p. 73.
6. *Ibid.*, p. 74.
7. L 171.
8. L 172.
9. L 185.
10. L 246.
11. L 172.
12. L 139.
13. L 74.
14. L 226.
15. L 137.

Notes

Chapter 11

1. L 72.
2. L 166.
3. L 74.
4. Prayer 11, on the Feast of the Annunciation.
5. L 342.
6. *Ibid.*
7. L 54; 52; 25.
8. L 29.
9. L 272; 64.
10. L 257.
11. L 24.
12. L 48.

Chapter 12

1. L 166.
2. L 154.
3. L 21.
4. L 22.
5. L 368.
6. L 206.
7. L 205.
8. D 45, p. 93.
9. Raymond, *Life*, #139.
10. L 344.
11. L 220; Raymond, *Life*, #137.
12. L 220.
13. L 226.
14. L 108.
15. L 226.
16. Rm 13:14; L 175.

Chapter 13

1. L 54.
2. L 36.
3. L 221.
4. L 35.
5. L 6.
6. D 13 & 15, pp. 49 & 54.
7. Mt 10:24.

8. L 221.
9. From the suppressed Feast of the Translation of St. Catherine.
10. L 26.
11. L 81.
12. L 262.
13. L 221.
14. L 81 & 112.
15. L 226.
16. L 215.
17. *Ibid.*
18. D 78, p. 147.
19. L 273.
20. *Ibid.*

Chapter 14

1. L 36.
2. L 146.
3. D 144, p. 301.
4. D 167, p. 364.
5. L 129.
6. D 165, p. 360.
7. D 167, p. 365-366.
8. L 226.
9. D 167, p. 366.
10. D 146, p. 307.
11. D 2, p. 27.

Chapter 15

1. L 84.
2. *Ibid.*
3. *Ibid.*
4. L 17.
5. L 62.
6. *Ibid.*
7. Dante, *Divine Comedy: Paradise*, XXIII, 67-69, p. 169.
8. L 139; 127.
9. L 275.
10. D 158, p. 335-338.
11. L 275.
12. *Ibid.*

13. L 35.
14. L 159. Here the word "portare" is used the first time in the sense of Dante's *Divine Comedy: Hell*, III, 88-89, p. 6; as "a means of transport." "Through other portals, you shall reach the shore."

Chapter 16

1. L 65.
2. D 44, p. 89.
3. *Ibid.*, pp. 89-90.
4. L 245.
5. *Ibid.*
6. *Ibid.*
7. D 102, p. 194.
8. D 135, p. 278; L 221.
9. *Ibid.*
10. L 221.
11. L 213.
12. D 146, p. 307.
13. D 139, p. 286.
14. D 146, p. 308.
15. *Ibid.*
16. D l47, pp. 310-311.
17. *Ibid.*, p. 310.